GROWING UP WITH QUILTS

15 Projects for Babies to Teens

Mimi Dietrich & Sally Schneider

Martingale ®
& C O M P A N Y

CREDITS

CEO: Daniel J. Martin
President: Nancy J. Martin
Publisher: Jane Hamada
Editorial Director: Mary V. Green
Managing Editor: Tina Cook
Technical Editor: Darra Williamson
Copy Editor: Durby Peterson
Design Director: Stan Green
Illustrator: Laurel Strand
Cover and Text Designer: Regina Girard
Photographer: Brent Kane

That Patchwork Place® is an imprint
of Martingale & Company®.

Growing Up with Quilts: 15 Projects for Babies to Teens
© 2004 by Mimi Dietrich and Sally Schneider

Martingale & Company
20205 144th Avenue NE
Woodinville, WA 98072-8478 USA
www.martingale-pub.com

Printed in China
09 08 07 06 05 04   8 7 6 5 4 3 2 1

MISSION STATEMENT

*Dedicated to providing quality products
and service to inspire creativity.*

Library of Congress Cataloging-in-Publication Data
Dietrich, Mimi.
   Growing up with quilts : 15 projects for babies to teens / Mimi Dietrich and Sally Schneider.
      p. cm.
   ISBN 1-56477-539-9
   1. Patchwork—Patterns. 2. Quilting. 3. Children's quilts. I. Schneider, Sally. II. Title.
   TT835 .D5297 2004
   746 .46 ' 041—dc22

                                           2004010484

DEDICATION

To our children, Jon and Ryan Dietrich, and David, Drew, and Ted Schneider. We look forward to making lots more quilts, this time for your children.

ACKNOWLEDGMENTS

We both had a lot of help from our friends on this book:
Bob Dietrich, who came up with the title.

Linda Newsom, Laurie Gregg, and Kate Sullivan, our fantastic machine quilters, who among them quilted all but one of the quilts.

Norma Campbell, who made "Treasure Baskets."

Kaitlin Scott, who transferred the photos onto fabric.

Emily Watson, Mimi's quilter's apprentice.

Karen Baker, who inspired "May Angels Watch Over You."

Sally Broeker, who drafted the letters for "Now I Know My ABCs."

Lauren Daniel, who had her friends sign "Hearts and Ribbons."

Andrea Warfel, our young "consultant."

Quilters Dream Cotton for providing their Select Loft batting.

The staff at Seminole Sampler Quilt Shop in Catonsville, Maryland, who are always patient and creative with color.

The wonderful editor, illustrator, designer, and photographer who made this book match our vision for it.

Karen Soltys, Mary Green, Terry Martin, and the rest of the staff at Martingale & Company.

Zachary and Alec Schneider, Sally's grandchildren, who inspire new designs all the time (without even knowing it!).

CONTENTS

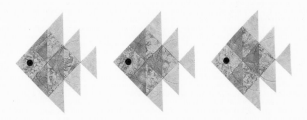

INTRODUCTION

What is your earliest comforting memory? Is it the cool sensation of satin binding sliding through your fingers, the fuzzy touch of chenille on your cheek, or the feel of a soft quilt? These are all fond memories we both share from our early childhood, and we want to pass them on to our children and grandchildren.

We have been friends for a long time. We met at a quilt show in 1990, and over the years our paths have continued to cross. We often talked about our sons and the quilts we made for them. Now that our boys are all grown up, and some of them are married, it's time to talk about grandchildren—and "grand quilts"!

We both made our first quilts when our first sons were born. As we stitched, we knew we were doing our best to welcome them into the world with our handmade quilts. Now that our children are grown, it's amazing to realize all of the quilts we've made for them: baby quilts, nap quilts for nursery school, big-boy-bed quilts, teenage quilts, graduation quilts, and wedding quilts. We are ready to do it again, this time for our grandchildren.

Ask any child, and many times he or she will tell you about a favorite quilt. Sally's grandson Zach can't go to sleep without his "blankys"—two of the quilts she made for him when he was born, plus the one she made when he got his big-boy bed. Even teenagers cuddle up with ragged, tattered remnants of their childhood quilt. Mimi's 25-year-old son,

Ryan, recently brought home his "heirloom 'Fish' quilt" from his collection.

If you are a new mom or seasoned granny, welcome your baby into the world as you make a special quilt. Think about creating a "Secret Garden" with lively, colorful flowers. Sing the nursery song "Itsy-Bitsy Spider," and teach your little one how the spider climbs up the water spout, or wish your baby good night with "Starlight, Starbright." Tuck her in and comfort her with "May Angels Watch Over You."

As babies grow into toddlers, teach them the alphabet with "Now I Know My ABCs." Play cars with your son as he settles down for his nap under "Beep, Beep." Wish your daughter "Good night, sleep tight," and assure her that these patchwork "Bed Bugs" won't bite.

Youngsters love to collect things, and what better place to hide their collections than in the pockets of "Treasure Baskets." Create a pieced-goldfish pond for the young naturalist with "Fantasy Fishes." Remember a favorite adventure at "Summer Camp" with patchwork mountains, trees, fish, and a few hidden bears. Let "Butterfly Kisses" be the perfect way to end the day.

Teenagers especially love new quilts. Their interests have grown and changed, and a new quilt reflects this exciting time in their life. The plain squares in "Hearts and Ribbons" are designed for collecting autographs at a sleepover or cheerleading camp. "Dreamweaver" and "Playing with Plaid" can be made either in school colors or those of a favorite sports team. "Scrapbook Memories" is perfect for displaying special photographs and memories of friends and family from all those childhood years. These would also be great graduation gifts, providing a touch of home when your student leaves for college.

Quilt shops are full of fabulous fabrics for children's quilts. There's a rainbow of bright colors, and there are fun novelty prints, soft pastels, and warm, cuddly flannels. There is a great selection to inspire any quiltmaker. Just for fun, take your child with you when you select fabrics for his or her quilt.

These quilts are made with a variety of techniques. Sally is a patchwork person, and Mimi is an appliqué person, so we thought we could present a good mix of patterns and designs. We even switched roles for a few projects: Mimi had a great time piecing, and Sally enjoyed a little appliqué!

Whether you are Grandma, Granny, Nana, Mom-Mom, Gran Gran, or Mom, we hope you enjoy our "Granny's Goodies." These are tips gleaned in our 60-plus (combined) years of quilting experience that will make your quilting easier, more accurate, or just more fun.

We hope you enjoy making these quilts as much as we did.

Mimi and Sally

STARLIGHT, STARBRIGHT

By Mimi Dietrich, Baltimore, Maryland, 2003.
Machine quilted by Linda Newsom, Crofton, Maryland.

When it's time to go to sleep at night, wrap your baby in a heavenly quilt and cuddle up in your favorite rocking chair. This "good-night" nursery quilt combines light and dark blues with bright gold and yellow—perfect for wishing on a star.

Finished Quilt Size: 48½" x 66½"

Finished Block Size: 9"

MATERIALS

Yardages are based on 42"-wide fabric.

2¾ yards of dark blue print for Nine Patch blocks and outer border

1½ yards of light blue print for Nine Patch blocks and binding

⅝ yard of bright gold print for Star blocks and inner border

¼ yard of yellow print for Star blocks

3 yards of fabric for backing

55" x 73" piece of batting

CUTTING

All measurements include ¼"-wide seam allowances.

From the light blue print, cut:

- 8 strips, 3½" x 40"
- 1 strip, 3½" x 40"; crosscut into 8 squares, 3½" x 3½"
- 1 strip, 4¼" x 40"; crosscut into 6 squares, 4¼" x 4¼". Cut twice diagonally to yield 24 quarter-square triangles.
- 7 binding strips, 2" x 40"

From the *lengthwise* grain of the dark blue print, cut:

- 2 border strips, 5½" x 56½" 60-62
- 2 border strips, 5½" x 48½" 50-02

From the remaining dark blue print, cut:

- 7 strips, 3½" x 40"
- 3 strips, 3½" x 40"; crosscut into 24 squares, 3½" x 3½"
- 2 squares, 4¼" x 4¼"; cut twice diagonally to yield 8 quarter-square triangles

From the bright gold print, cut:

- 5 border strips, 1½" x 40"
- 1 strip, 3½" x 40"; crosscut into 8 squares, 3½" x 3½"
- 2 strips, 4¼" x 40"; crosscut into 16 squares, 4¼" x 4¼". Cut twice diagonally to yield 64 quarter-square triangles.

From the yellow print, cut:

- 1 strip, 4¼" x 40"; crosscut into 8 squares, 4¼" x 4¼". Cut twice diagonally to yield 32 quarter-square triangles.

MAKING NINE PATCH BLOCKS

You need 16 Nine Patch blocks: 6 of Nine Patch A and 10 of Nine Patch B. Refer to "Making Strip Sets" on page 85 as needed.

1. Sew a 3½"-wide light blue strip between two 3½"-wide dark blue strips; press. Make two strip sets. Crosscut into 22 segments, each 3½" wide.

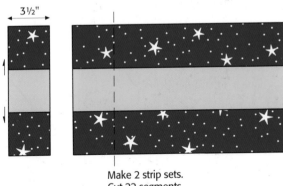

Make 2 strip sets.
Cut 22 segments.

2. Sew a 3½"-wide dark blue strip between two 3½"-wide light blue strips; press. Make three strip sets. Crosscut into 26 segments, each 3½" wide.

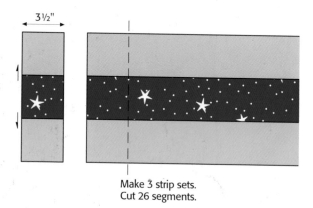

Make 3 strip sets.
Cut 26 segments.

3. Sew one segment from step 2 between two segments from step 1; press. Make six and label them Nine Patch A.

Nine Patch A
Make 6. A

4. Sew one segment from step 1 between two segments from step 2; press. Make 10 and label them Nine Patch B.

Nine Patch B
Make 10. B

MAKING STAR BLOCKS

You need eight Star blocks for this quilt; two of Star A and six of Star B.

1. Sew bright gold triangles and yellow triangles together in pairs; press. Make 32.

Make 32.

2. Sew bright gold triangles and dark blue triangles together in pairs; press. Make eight. Sew each unit to a unit from step 1; press. Make eight.

Make 8.

3. Arrange four units from step 2, four light blue squares, and one bright gold square as shown. Sew the units and squares into rows; press. Sew the rows together; press. Make two and label them Star A.

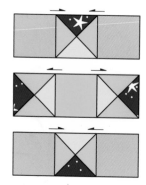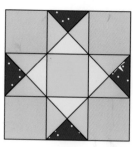

Star A
Make 2. A

4. Sew bright gold triangles and light blue triangles together in pairs; press. Make 24. Sew each unit to a unit from step 1; press. Make 24.

Make 24.

5. Arrange four units from step 4, four dark blue squares, and one bright gold square as shown. Sew the units and squares into rows; press. Sew the rows together; press. Make six and label them Star B.

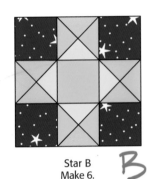

Star B
Make 6.

ASSEMBLING THE QUILT

1. Arrange the Nine Patch and Star blocks in six rows of four blocks each as shown in the quilt layout at right. Take care to place the A and B blocks correctly.

2. Sew the blocks together into rows; press the seams in opposite directions from row to row.

3. Sew the rows together; press.

4. Sew the bright gold print strips end to end with diagonal seams to make one continuous border strip. Measure the quilt through the center from top to bottom and cut two strips to that measurement. Sew the strips to the sides of the quilt. Press the seams toward the strips.

5. Measure the quilt from side to side, including the strips you've just added. Cut two strips to that measurement and sew them to the top and bottom of the quilt; press.

6. Sew the 5½" x 56½" dark blue strips to the sides of the quilt, and the 5½" x 48½" dark blue strips to the top and bottom. Press the seams toward the dark blue strips.

Quilt Layout

FINISHING

Refer to pages 90–95 of "Basic Quiltmaking Techniques" as needed.

1. Mark the quilt top with a quilting design of your choice.

2. Cut the backing fabric crosswise into two equal lengths, remove the selvages, and sew the pieces together to make a backing with a horizontal seam. Trim the backing so that it is approximately 6" larger than the quilt top.

3. Layer the quilt top with the batting and backing; baste.

4. Hand or machine quilt as desired.

5. Trim the excess batting and backing even with the edges of the quilt top and attach a hanging sleeve, if desired. Join the light blue binding strips with diagonal seams; bind the edges of the quilt.

6. Label your quilt.

SECRET GARDEN

By Sally Schneider, Albuquerque, New Mexico, 2003.
Machine quilted by Linda Newsom, Crofton, Maryland.

Blue skies, brilliant sunshine, and colorful flowers swaying in the breeze—what more could any little girl want in a quilt for her bed? You can transform the flowers into your little girl's favorites by using different colors for the Pinwheel blocks.

Finished quilt size: 40" x 60"
Finished block size: 6"

Granny's Goodies

Select blue, yellow, and green prints in a value gradation from light to dark for sky, sunshine, and grass.

MATERIALS

Yardages are based on 42"-wide fabric.

1⅛ yards of light blue background print for blocks and sky

1⅛ yards of medium blue print #1 for sky, outer border, and binding

½ yard of light yellow print for blocks, sunshine, and inner border

⅜ yard of medium green print #1 for grass and stems

¼ yard *each* of medium and dark yellow, red, dark pink, purple, and light and dark orange prints for blocks

¼ yard *each* of 3 assorted green prints for grass: light, medium green #2, and dark

¼ yard *each* of 3 assorted blue prints for sky: light, medium blue #2, and dark blue

2½ yards of fabric for backing

46" x 66" piece of batting

CUTTING

All measurements include ¼"-wide seam allowances.

From the light blue background print, cut:

- 2 strips, 4¼" x 40"; crosscut into 11 squares, 4¼" x 4¼". Cut twice diagonally to yield 44 quarter-square triangles.
- 1 strip, 3⅞" x 40"; crosscut into 5 squares, 3⅞" x 3⅞". Cut once diagonally to yield 10 half-square triangles. (You will have 1 extra triangle.)
- 3 strips, 6½" x 40"; crosscut into:
    14 pieces, 3½" x 6½"
    2 squares, 6½" x 6½"
    2 pieces, 6½" x 12½"
- 1 strip, 3½" x 40"; crosscut into 2 rectangles, 3½" x 12½", and 2 squares, 3½" x 3½"

From the light yellow print, cut:

- 2 squares, 4¼" x 4¼"; cut twice diagonally to yield 8 quarter-square triangles
- 5 squares, 3⅞" x 3⅞"; cut once diagonally to yield 10 half-square triangles. (You will have 1 extra triangle.)
- 5 border strips, 1½" x 40"

From the medium yellow print, cut:

- 2 squares, 4¼" x 4¼"; cut twice diagonally to yield 8 quarter-square triangles
- 4 squares, 3⅞" x 3⅞"; cut once diagonally to yield 8 half-square triangles

From the dark yellow print, cut:

- 1 square, 4¼" x 4¼"; cut twice diagonally to yield 4 quarter-square triangles
- 2 squares, 3⅞" x 3⅞"; cut once diagonally to yield 4 half-square triangles

From the light orange print, cut:
- 2 squares, 4¼" x 4¼"; cut twice diagonally to yield 8 quarter-square triangles
- 2 squares, 3⅞" x 3⅞"; cut once diagonally to yield 4 half-square triangles.

From the dark orange print, cut:
- 1 square, 4¼" x 4¼"; cut twice diagonally to yield 4 quarter-square triangles
- 2 squares, 3⅞" x 3⅞"; cut once diagonally to yield 4 half-square triangles

From the purple print, cut:
- 3 squares, 4¼" x 4¼"; cut twice diagonally to yield 12 quarter-square triangles

From the red print, cut:
- 6 squares, 3⅞" x 3⅞"; cut once diagonally to yield 12 half-square triangles

From the dark pink print, cut:
- 6 squares, 3⅞" x 3⅞"; cut once diagonally to yield 12 half-square triangles

From the medium green print #1, cut:
- 1 strip, 11" x 40". Cut 9 bias strips, 1" wide. From the remainder, cut 7 squares, 3½" x 3½".

From medium blue print #1, cut:
- 1 strip, 3½" x 40"; crosscut into 7 squares, 3½" x 3½"
- 5 border strips, 4¼" x 40"
- 6 binding strips, 2¼" x 40"

From each of the light blue, medium blue #2, and dark blue prints, cut:
- 1 strip, 3½" x 40"; crosscut into 7 squares, 3½" x 3½" (21 total)

From the medium green print #2, cut:
- 1 strip, 3½" x 40"; crosscut into 7 squares, 3½" x 3½"

From each of the light green and dark green prints, cut:
- 1 strip, 3½" x 40"; crosscut into 8 squares, 3½" x 3½" (16 total)

MAKING PINWHEEL BLOCKS AND SUNSHINE UNITS

You need 11 Pinwheel blocks made in various combinations of fabrics. The method below describes the most efficient way to put the blocks together and allows for the most flexibility in color arrangement.

1. Sew a blue background quarter-square triangle to each light yellow, medium yellow, dark yellow, light orange, dark orange, and purple quarter-square triangle as shown below; press. Make 44 total.

Make 44.

2. Select four matching triangle units from step 1 and four matching medium yellow, dark yellow, light orange, dark orange, red, or dark pink half-square triangles. Sew a unit and half-square triangle together as shown; press. Make 44, in matching sets of 4.

Make 44.

3. Arrange four matching units as shown.

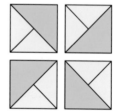

4. Sew the units into rows; press. Sew the rows together, carefully matching the points in the center. Undo the next-to-last seam from the

raw edge to the seam intersection, and then press as shown. Make 11 blocks.

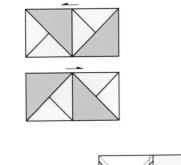

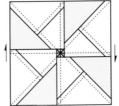
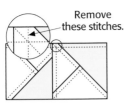

Remove these stitches.

Make 2.

Make 1.

Make 1.

Make 2.

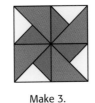
Make 3.

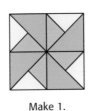
Make 1.

Make 1.

5. Sew the blue background half-square triangles and light yellow half-square triangles together as shown; press. Make nine sunshine units.

Make 9.

ASSEMBLING THE QUILT

1. Turn under both long edges of each medium green print #1 bias strip and press.

2. Arrange the Pinwheel blocks; sunshine units; 3½" x 6½", 3½" x 12½", 6½" square, and 6½" x 12½" background pieces; background, medium blue print #1, medium blue print #2, light blue, and dark blue 3½" squares; and medium green print #1, medium green print #2, light green, and dark green 3½" squares as shown in the diagram below. (You will have some 3½" squares left over.)

3. Pin a bias strip to the bottom of each Pinwheel block except the yellow (sun) Pinwheel block in the upper-left corner.

4. Assemble the quilt sections as shown, pressing as you go. Sew the bias strip in the seam at the bottom of each Pinwheel block either as the section is assembled or as the sections are sewn together. Make six sections.

5. Sew the sections together, leaving the ends of the bias strips hanging free; press.

6. Position the bias strips as desired; pin. Refer to "Appliqué" on page 86 and stitch the strips to the background. Undo a bit of the seam where each strip ends, tuck the end into the seam, and restitch the seam.

7. Sew the light yellow strips end to end with diagonal seams to make one continuous border strip. Measure the quilt through the center from top to bottom and cut two strips to that measurement. Sew the strips to the sides of the quilt. Press the seams toward the strips.

8. Measure the quilt from side to side, including the strips you've just added. Cut two strips to that measurement and sew them to the top and bottom of the quilt; press.

9. Sew the 4¼"-wide medium blue print #1 strips end to end with diagonal seams to make one continuous border strip. Repeat steps 7 and 8 to measure, trim, and sew the strips to the sides, top, and bottom of the quilt. Press the seams toward the blue strips.

FINISHING

Refer to pages 90–95 of "Basic Quiltmaking Techniques" as needed.

1. Mark the quilt top with a quilting design of your choice.

2. Cut the backing fabric crosswise into two equal lengths, remove the selvages, and sew the pieces together to make a backing with a horizontal seam. Trim the backing so that it is approximately 6" larger than the quilt top.

3. Layer the quilt top with backing and batting; baste.

4. Hand or machine quilt as desired.

5. Trim the excess batting and backing even with the edges of the quilt top and attach a hanging sleeve, if desired. Join the medium blue print #1 binding strips with diagonal seams; bind the edges of the quilt.

6. Label your quilt.

Quilt Layout

MAY ANGELS
WATCH OVER YOU

Pieced, appliquéd, and quilted by Mimi Dietrich, Baltimore, Maryland, 2002.

Favorite nighttime childhood poems tell of the moon, the stars, sheep to count, and angels who watch over us. Vintage hand-appliqué patterns inspired the angels in this darling quilt; they are embellished with embroidery, buttons, beads, and a touch of dimensional appliqué. If you prefer, use fusible appliqué techniques and machine stitches to decorate the angels instead. "May angels watch over you" as you stitch, and protect your special child through the night.

Finished quilt size: 48½" x 62½"

Finished block size: 8½"

Granny's Goodies

If you embellish your quilt with buttons and beads, use it as a wall hanging rather than on the crib or toddler's bed. Buttons and beads can be dangerous for little ones.

MATERIALS

Yardages are based on 42"-wide fabric.

3 yards of blue print for blocks, letter appliqués, dogtooth border, and binding

2¾ yards of floral print for outer border, setting squares, and setting triangles

¼ yard of tan check (or desired color) for face and feet appliqués

¼ yard of light brown print (or desired color) for hair

Assorted plaid and check scraps for halo and dress appliqués

Assorted colorful print scraps for accessory appliqués and hankies

3¼ yards of fabric for backing

55" x 69" piece of batting

12 scalloped doilies (4" diameter) for angel wings

Black and ecru embroidery floss

24 black beads for angel eyes

Assorted small buttons for embellishment

Freezer paper

CUTTING

All measurements include ¼"-wide seam allowances. See pages 17–19 for appliqué cutting instructions.

From the *lengthwise* grain of the blue print, cut:
- 4 strips, 2" x 48½"
- 2 strips, 2" x 62½"
- 2 strips, 2" x 36½"

From the remaining blue print, cut:
- 3 strips, 9" x 40"; crosscut into 12 squares, 9" x 9"
- 6 binding strips, 2" x 40"

From the light brown print, cut:
- 12 strips, 1⅛" x 14"

From the *lengthwise* grain of the floral print, cut:
- 3 border strips, 6½" x 48½"
- 1 border strip, 8½" x 48½"

From the remaining floral print, cut:
- 2 strips, 9" x 40"; crosscut into 6 squares, 9" x 9"
- 3 squares, 13¼" x 13¼"; cut twice diagonally to yield 12 quarter-square triangles (You will have 2 extra triangles.)
- 2 squares, 6⅞" x 6⅞"; cut once diagonally to yield 4 half-square triangles

MAKING ANGEL BLOCKS

You need 12 Angel blocks. Mimi appliquéd this heirloom quilt by hand. You can use your favorite technique. Refer to "Appliqué" on pages 86–88 as needed and adapt and reverse patterns as necessary.

1. Use the patterns on page 20 to make templates for appliqués B–H. Cut 12 *each* of appliqué pieces B, C, and F from the tan (or desired color) check, and 12 *each* of appliqué pieces D, E, G, and H from the assorted plaids and checks.

2. Use the pattern on page 20 to center and trace the angel on each 9" blue print square. Do not trace the square (I) in the angel's hand. Note that the angel is placed diagonally on the block. Make 12.

Make 12.

3. Use the patterns on page 21 to make templates for each of the 12 small designs. Trace a different design in the square (I) in each angel's hand, and then use the templates to cut the appliqués from assorted colorful scraps.

4. Place a doily in the wing area (A) of each marked block as shown. Appliqué the two top scallops. Trim the excess doily so that it overlaps the angel's dress (D) by ¼".

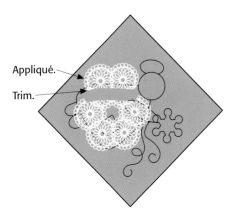

Appliqué.
Trim.

5. Appliqué pieces B–F and piece H (in alphabetical order) to the blocks. Appliqué the bottom (curved) edge of piece G. Cut and fold a 1½" square of contrasting fabric as shown. Tuck the raw edges into the pocket, and sew across the top of the pocket to secure.

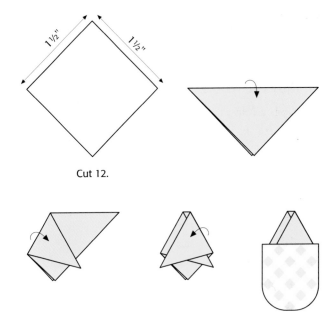

1½"   1½"

Cut 12.

6. Appliqué a small design from step 3 in each angel's hand.

7. Fold the long edges of each 1⅛"-wide light brown (or desired color) strip to the center of

the strip, wrong sides together, so that the raw edges meet; press. Make 12.

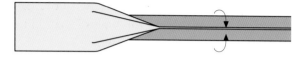

8. Lay each strip right side up along the ruching guide on page 20. Use a fabric marker to mark the dots on the folded edges of the strip at staggered 1" intervals. Sew a running stitch by hand from dot to dot as shown. Make 12.

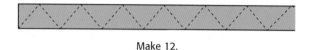

Make 12.

9. Pull the thread to gather the fabric into a 4" strip, leaving a ¼" "tail" at each end. Fold the tails under, and then appliqué the edges around each angel's head as shown.

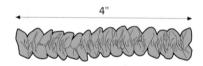

4"

10. Use black embroidery floss and a blanket stitch to outline the appliqués (except for the hair and wings). Refer to the pattern on page 20. Use ecru floss and a chain stitch to embroider the swirls.

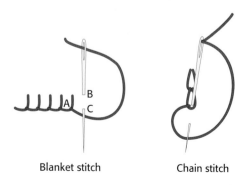

Blanket stitch   Chain stitch

11. Sew two black beads to each angel's face for eyes. If desired, refer to the photo on page 15 to add small button embellishments to the blocks.

APPLIQUÉING THE BORDERS

1. Trace the dogtooth border pattern on page 23 onto freezer paper until you have patterns long enough to fit the quilt borders. You need two strips with 18 triangle points and two strips with 24 triangle points for the inner dogtooth borders, and two strips with 24 points and two strips with 31 points for the outer dogtooth borders.

2. Iron the freezer paper to the right side of the appropriately sized 2"-wide blue strips.

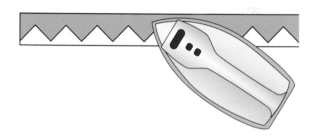

3. Fold the 8½" x 48½" (top) and one 6½" x 48½" (bottom) floral strip in half to find the center point of each strip. Align an "inside" freezer paper/fabric strip (freezer-paper side face up) along the raw edge of each floral strip so that there are nine teeth on either side of the center point. Pin, and then baste in place.

4. Repeat step 3 with the two remaining 6½" x 48½" floral strips, this time placing the freezer paper/fabric strips so that there are 12 teeth on either side of the center point.

5. Trim the blue fabric around the edge of the freezer paper, leaving a ¼" seam allowance as shown. Needle turn the seam allowance under the freezer paper to appliqué the edges in place. Remove the freezer paper. Repeat for all four borders. Do not add the outer freezer paper/fabric strips at this time.

6. Use the patterns on pages 22–23 to make templates for the letter appliqués. Cut each letter from the remaining blue print. Refer to the quilt photo on page 15. With the dogtooth strip on the bottom, appliqué the letters to the top (8½" x 48½") border. Outline each letter with black embroidery floss and a blanket stitch.

ASSEMBLING THE QUILT

1. Arrange the Angel blocks, 9" floral squares, quarter-square side setting triangles, and half-square corner setting triangles in diagonal rows as shown below. Take care to place each Angel block in the proper place.
2. Sew the blocks, squares, and setting triangles together in diagonal rows. Press the seams away from the Angel blocks.
3. Sew the rows together; press.

ADDING BORDERS

1. Refer to the photo on page 15. With the dogtooth edges next to the quilt, sew a 6½" x 48½" floral border strip to the sides of the quilt. Press the seams toward the border.
2. Sew a 6½" x 48½" floral border strip to the bottom of the quilt, taking care to match the triangle intersections where the borders meet. (If you wish, you can cover the intersection with a blue button later!) Sew the 8½" x 48½" border strip to the top of the quilt.
3. Appliqué the remaining blue dogtooth strips to the outer edges of the quilt. There should be 24 teeth along the top and bottom edges, and 31 teeth along the sides.

FINISHING

Refer to pages 90–95 of "Basic Quiltmaking Techniques" as needed.

1. Mark the quilt top with a quilting design of your choice.
2. Cut the backing fabric crosswise into two equal lengths, remove the selvages, and sew the pieces together to make a backing with a horizontal seam. Trim the backing so that it is approximately 6" larger than the quilt top.
3. Layer the quilt top with the batting and backing; baste.
4. Hand or machine quilt as desired.
5. Trim the excess batting and backing even with the edges of the quilt top and attach a hanging sleeve, if desired. Join the blue print binding strips with diagonal seams; bind the edges of the quilt.
6. Refer to the photo on page 15 and sew small beads and buttons to the quilt as embellishment. Make sure they are attached securely.
7. Label your quilt.

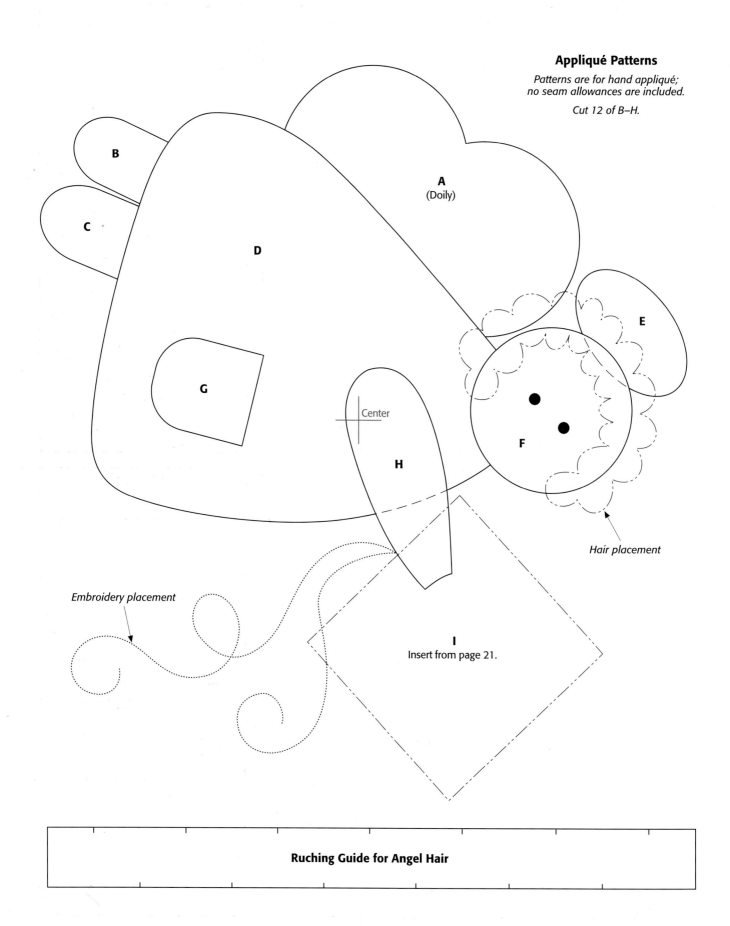

Appliqué Patterns

*Patterns are for hand appliqué;
no seam allowances are included.*

Cut 12 of B–H.

B

C

D

A
(Doily)

G

E

F

Center

H

Hair placement

Embroidery placement

I
Insert from page 21.

Ruching Guide for Angel Hair

Dogtooth Border

ITSY-BITSY SPIDER

By Sally Schneider, Albuquerque, New Mexico, 2003.
Machine quilted by Laurie Gregg, Ellicott City, Maryland.

If you have ever sung "Itsy-Bitsy Spider" to your child or grandchild and done the hand motions that accompany the words, you might see a similar pattern in the placement of the light background fabric in this quilt. Pairs of colors, one dark and one medium, give the blocks depth and movement.

*Spiders · maroon
yellow
green
Blue*

Finished quilt size: 43" x 59"

Finished block size: 8"

MATERIALS

Yardages are based on 42"-wide fabric.

2 yards of white-on-white print for block background — *cream*

¾ yard of green print for outer border

⅝ yard of dark purple print for blocks and binding

⅜ yard of yellow print for inner border

⅜ yard *each* of medium value prints in green, orange, purple, blue, and pink for blocks

¼ yard *each* of dark value prints in green, orange, blue, and pink for blocks

2¾ yards of fabric for backing

49" x 65" piece of batting

CUTTING

All measurements include ¼"-wide seam allowances.

From the dark purple print, cut:
- 2 strips, 2½" x 40"; crosscut into 20 squares, 2½" x 2½"
- 6 binding strips, 2¼" x 40"

From the white-on-white print, cut: *(cream)*
- 7 strips, 4½" x 40"; crosscut into 100 rectangles, 2½" x 4½"
- 13 strips, 2½" x 40"; crosscut into 200 squares, 2½" x 2½"

From *each* medium print, cut:
- 2 strips, 4½" x 40"; crosscut into 20 rectangles, 2½" x 4½" (100 total)

From *each* dark print, cut:
- 2 strips, 2½" x 40"; crosscut into 20 squares, 2½" x 2½" (80 total)

From the yellow print, cut:
- 5 border strips, 2" x 40"

From the green print, cut:
- 5 border strips, 4¼" x 40"

MAKING SEESAW BLOCKS

You need 24 Seesaw blocks. To make construction easier, you will make five blocks in each color.

Granny's Goodies

Why not save the extra Seesaw block to use for the label?

1. Refer to "Sewing Folded Corners" on page 85. Sew a 2½" dark purple square to the right edge of a 2½" x 4½" white rectangle as shown; trim and press. Make 20.

Make 20.

2. Sew two 2½" white squares to each medium purple 2½" x 4½" rectangle as shown; trim and press. Make 20.

Make 20.

3. Sew a unit from step 1 and step 2 together as shown; press. Make 20.

Make 20.

4. Arrange four units as shown. Sew the units into rows; press. Sew the rows together, carefully matching the points in the center; press. Make five.

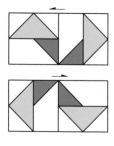
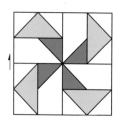

Make 5.

5. Repeat steps 1–4, substituting a different color for the medium and dark purple rectangles and squares. Make five blocks in each color.

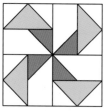
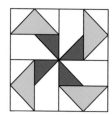

Make 5.   Make 5.

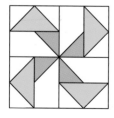
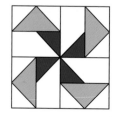

Make 5.   Make 5.

ASSEMBLING THE QUILT

1. Arrange the blocks in six rows of four blocks each, arranging the colors in diagonal rows as shown in the quilt layout above right.

2. Sew the blocks together into rows. Press the seams in opposite directions from row to row.

3. Sew the rows together; press.

4. Sew the yellow strips end to end with diagonal seams to make one continuous border strip. Measure the quilt through the center from top to bottom and cut two strips to that measurement. Sew the strips to the sides of the quilt. Press the seams toward the strips.

5. Measure the quilt from side to side, including the strips you've just added. Cut two strips to

that measurement and sew them to the top and bottom of the quilt; press.

6. Sew the green strips end to end with diagonal seams to make one continuous border strip. Repeat steps 4 and 5 to measure, trim, and sew the strips to the sides, top, and bottom of the quilt. Press the seams toward the green strips.

Quilt Layout

FINISHING

Refer to pages 90–95 of "Basic Quiltmaking Techniques" as needed.

1. Mark the quilt top with a quilting design of your choice.

2. Cut the backing fabric crosswise into two equal lengths, remove the selvages, and sew the pieces together to make a backing with a horizontal seam. Trim the backing so that it is approximately 6" larger than the quilt top.

3. Layer the quilt top with the batting and backing; baste.

4. Hand or machine quilt as desired.

5. Trim the excess batting and backing even with the edges of the quilt top and attach a hanging sleeve, if desired. Join the dark purple binding strips with diagonal seams; bind the edges of the quilt.

6. Label your quilt.

BEEP, BEEP

By Mimi Dietrich, Baltimore, Maryland, 2003.
Machine quilted by Linda Newsom, Crofton, Maryland.

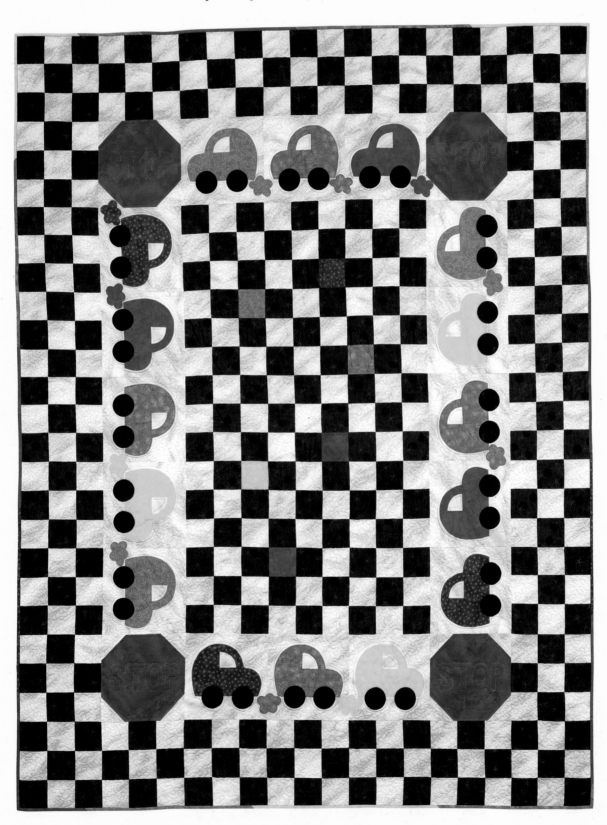

Brightly colored appliqué cars and checkered racing flags of black-and-white patchwork are sure to delight your favorite little boy. A white background fabric printed with gray streaks adds a sense of motion and makes a practical choice for a little boy's room.

Finished quilt size: 63½" x 81½"
Finished block size: 9"

MATERIALS

Yardages are based on 42"-wide fabric.

3⅜ yards of white-and-gray print for Nine Patch blocks, Stop Sign blocks, and appliqué background

2 yards of black print for Nine Patch blocks

¾ yard of red print for Nine Patch blocks, Stop Sign blocks, and binding

½ yard of black solid for wheel appliqués

⅜ yard *each* of bright value prints in orange, yellow, blue, green, and purple for car and smoke puff appliqués, Nine Patch blocks, and binding

5 yards of fabric for backing

70" x 88" piece of batting

CUTTING

All measurements include ¼"-wide seam allowances. See page 29 for appliqué cutting instructions.

From the white-and-gray print, cut:
- 4 strips, 9½" x 40"; crosscut into 16 squares, 9½" x 9½"
- 2 strips, 3¼" x 40"; crosscut into 16 squares, 3¼" x 3¼"
- 19 strips, 3½" x 40"

From the black print, cut:
- 19 strips, 3½" x 40"

From the red print, cut:
- 1 strip, 9½" x 40"; crosscut into 4 squares, 9½" x 9½"
- 1 square, 3½" x 3½"
- 3 binding strips, 2" x 20"

From *each* bright-print fabric, cut:
- 1 square, 3½" x 3½" (5 total)
- 3 binding strips, 2" x 20" (15 total)

MAKING NINE PATCH BLOCKS

You need 43 Nine Patch blocks: 22 of Nine Patch A, 15 of Nine Patch B, and 6 of Nine Patch C. Refer to "Making Strip Sets" on page 85 as needed.

1. Sew a 3½"-wide white-and-gray strip between two 3½"-wide black print strips; press. Make six strip sets. Crosscut into 65 segments, each 3½" wide.

Make 6 strip sets.
Cut 65 segments.

2. Sew a 3½"-wide black print strip between two 3½"-wide white-and-gray strips; press. Make six strip sets. Crosscut into 58 segments, each 3½" wide.

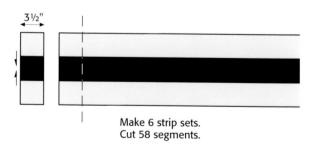

Make 6 strip sets.
Cut 58 segments.

3. Sew one segment from step 2 between two segments from step 1; press. Make 22 and label them Nine Patch A.

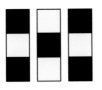

Nine Patch A
Make 22.

4. Sew one segment from step 1 between two segments from step 2; press. Make 15 and label them Nine Patch B.

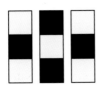

Nine Patch B
Make 15.

5. Sew a 3½"-wide black print strip to a 3½"-wide white-and-gray strip; press. Crosscut into six segments, each 3½"-wide. Sew a different 3½" red- or bright-print square to each segment as shown. Make six.

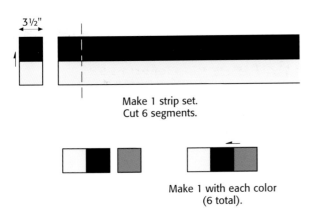

Make 1 strip set.
Cut 6 segments.

Make 1 with each color
(6 total).

6. Sew one segment from step 1 between a segment from step 2 and a segment from step 5 as shown; press. Make six and label them Nine Patch C.

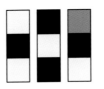

Nine Patch C
Make 1 with each color
(6 total).

MAKING STOP SIGN BLOCKS

Refer to "Sewing Folded Corners" on page 85. Sew a 3¼" white-and-gray square to each corner of a 9½" red square as shown; trim and press. Make 4.

Make 4.

APPLIQUÉING THE CAR BLOCKS

Mimi fused the appliqués to the background and finished the edges with the buttonhole stitch on her sewing machine. You can use your favorite technique. Refer to "Appliqué" on pages 86–88 as needed and adapt and reverse the patterns as necessary.

1. Use the patterns on page 31 to make templates for the car, wheel, and smoke puff appliqués. Cut 2 regular and 1 reverse car *each* from the orange and blue prints; 3 regular and 1 reverse car from the green print; and 3 regular cars *each* from the yellow and purple prints. Cut 3 smoke puffs *each* from the orange and green prints; 2 smoke puffs *each* from the blue and yellow prints; and 1 smoke puff from the purple print. Cut 32 wheels from the black solid.

2. Use the car pattern to trace the car onto each 9½" white-and-gray square. Reverse the pattern for 13 cars so that they face to the right of the block.

3. Refer to the photo on page 27 and the quilt layout on page 30. Appliqué the cars and wheels to the blocks as shown.

ASSEMBLING THE QUILT

1. Arrange the Nine Patch, Stop Sign, and Car blocks in nine rows of seven blocks each as shown in the quilt layout below. Take care to place the Nine Patch blocks—particularly Nine Patch C—correctly.

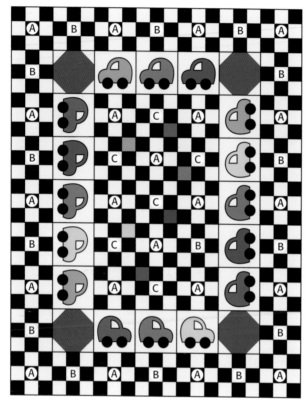

Quilt Layout

2. Sew the blocks together into rows; press the seams in opposite directions from row to row.

3. Sew the rows together; press.

4. Refer to the photo on page 27 and appliqué the smoke puffs behind the cars as shown.

FINISHING

Refer to pages 90–95 of "Basic Quiltmaking Techniques" as needed.

1. Mark the quilt top with a quilting design of your choice. If you wish, transfer the pattern below to quilt "STOP" in each Stop Sign block.

2. Cut the backing fabric crosswise into two equal lengths, remove the selvages, and sew the pieces together to make a backing with a vertical seam. Trim the backing so that it is approximately 6" larger than the quilt top.

3. Layer the quilt top with the batting and backing; baste.

4. Hand or machine quilt as desired.

5. Trim the excess batting and backing even with the edges of the quilt top and attach a hanging sleeve, if desired. Arrange the red- and bright-print binding strips rainbow fashion and join them with diagonal seams. Bind the edges of the quilt.

6. Label your quilt.

Quilting Design

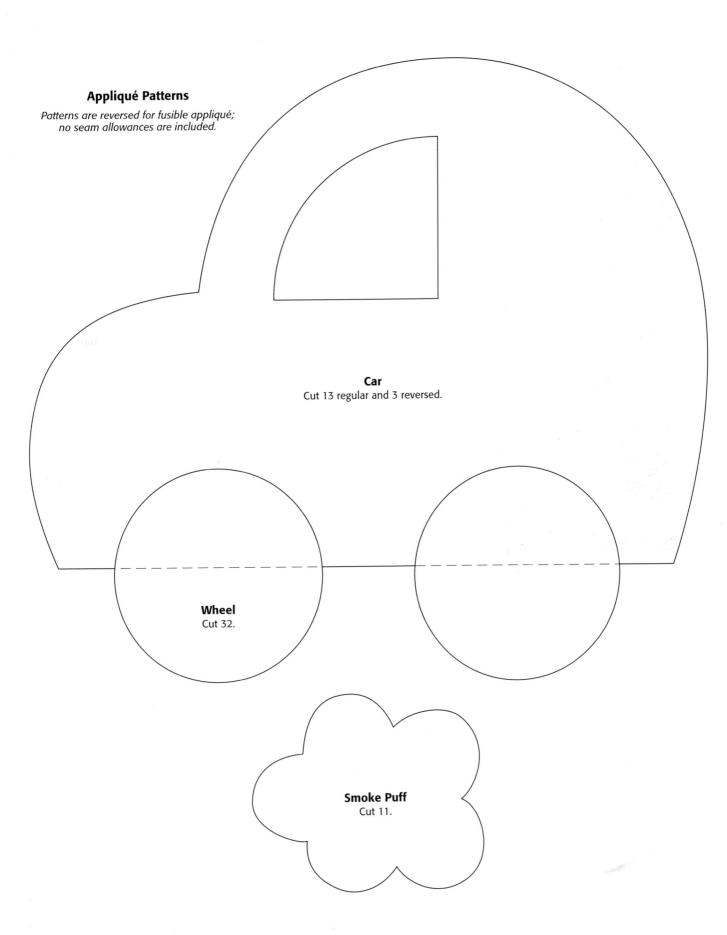

Appliqué Patterns

*Patterns are reversed for fusible appliqué;
no seam allowances are included.*

Car
Cut 13 regular and 3 reversed.

Wheel
Cut 32.

Smoke Puff
Cut 11.

NOW I KNOW MY ABCs

By Sally Schneider, Albuquerque, New Mexico, 2003.
Machine quilted by Kate Sullivan, Puyallup, Washington.

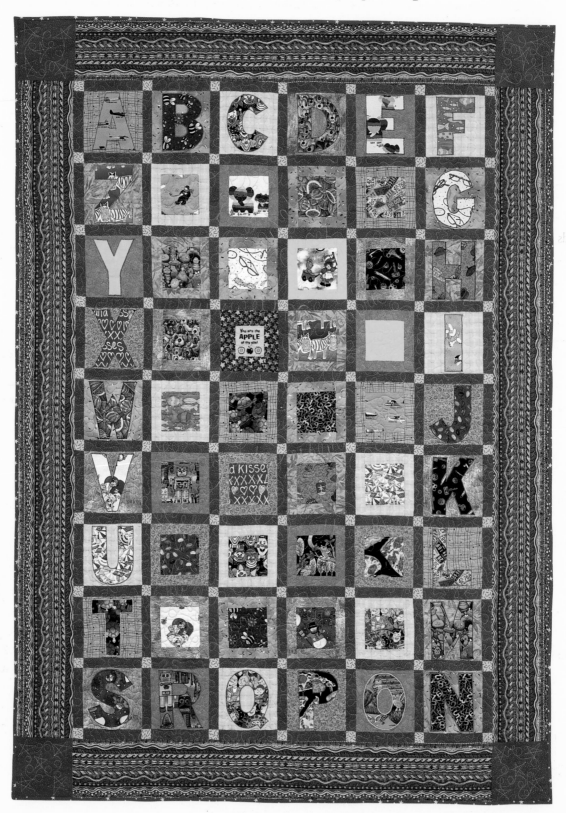

Start your fabric search now! In this alphabet quilt, you'll cut each appliqué from a novelty print that features a motif beginning with that letter. The pieced blocks are made from squares of the same novelty print framed with the fabric used for the appliqué background. What a great way for a child to learn to match colors, prints, sounds, and letters!

Finished quilt size: 55" x 76"

Finished block size: 6"

MATERIALS

Yardages are based on 42"-wide fabric.

1⅞ yards of multicolored stripe for border★

1¼ yards of red print #1 for sashing and border corner squares

½ yard *each* of seven tone-on-tone prints for Alphabet and Novelty blocks

¼ yard of yellow print for corner squares

6" x 10" piece *each* of 28 novelty prints—one starting with each letter of the alphabet plus two extra, for letter appliqués and Novelty blocks

4¾ yards of fabric for backing

½ yard of red print #2 for binding

61" x 82" piece of batting

1½ yards of fusible web

★ *If you prefer not to use a stripe and would rather have crosscut borders, you need only 1¼ yards.*

CUTTING

All measurements include ¼"-wide seam allowances. See page 34 for appliqué cutting instructions.

From *each* tone-on-tone print, cut:

- 1 strip, 6½" x 40"; crosscut into 4 squares, 6½" x 6½" (28 total; you will have 2 extra squares.)
- 3 strips, 1½" x 40"; crosscut into 8 strips, 1½" x 4½" (56 total), and 8 strips, 1½" x 6½" (56 total)

From *each* novelty print, cut:

- 1 square, 4½" x 4½" (28 total)

From red print #1, cut:

- 5 strips, 6½" x 40"; crosscut into 123 strips, 1½" x 6½"
- 1 strip, 6¼" x 40"; crosscut into 4 squares, 6¼" x 6¼"

From the yellow print, cut:

- 3 strips, 1½" x 40"; crosscut into 70 squares, 1½" x 1½"

From the *lengthwise* grain of the multicolored stripe, cut:

- 4 border strips, 6¼" x 67"★

From red print #2, cut:

- 7 binding strips, 2¼" x 40"

★ *If you prefer borders cut from the crosswise grain, cut 6 strips, 6¼" x 40".*

Granny's Goodies

Before fusing the letters, arrange the background squares on a design wall or other flat surface to make sure you have a good balance of color. If you don't preview the arrangement, you may get too many similar colors side by side.

MAKING ALPHABET BLOCKS

You need 26 Alphabet blocks. Sally fused the appliqués to the tone-on-tone background blocks. She finished the edges with the satin stitch on her sewing machine, using a variety of thread colors that contrast with both the letters and the backgrounds. You can use your favorite technique. Refer to "Appliqué" on pages 86–88 as needed and adapt and reverse the patterns as necessary.

1. Use the patterns on pages 36–37 to make templates for the letter appliqués, enlarging them as instructed. Cut each letter from the appropriate remaining novelty fabric—not the 4½" squares.

2. Refer to the photo on page 32 and the quilt layout on page 35. Appliqué each letter to a 6½" square of tone-on-tone print as shown. Make 26.

MAKING NOVELTY BLOCKS

You need 28 Novelty blocks. Sew each 4½" square of novelty print between two 1½" x 4½" strips of the tone-on-tone print that matches its letter background as shown; press. Sew the 1½" x 6½" strips to the remaining sides; press. Make 28.

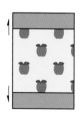 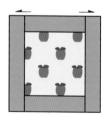

ASSEMBLING THE QUILT

Note: The alphabet begins in the upper-left corner and runs clockwise around the quilt top.

1. Refer to the photo on page 32 and the quilt layout on page 35. Arrange Alphabet blocks A–F and seven 1½" x 6½" red print #1 strips to make a row. Sew the blocks and strips together. Press the seams toward the strips. Repeat for Alphabet blocks S, R, Q, P, O, and N; press.

2. Repeat step 1 using two Alphabet blocks, four Novelty blocks, and seven red print #1 strips; press. Make seven rows.

3. Sew six red print #1 strips and seven 1½" yellow print squares to make a row. Press the seams toward the strips. Make 10.

Make 10.

4. Refer to the photo and layout. Arrange the rows from steps 1–3 as shown. Sew the rows together; press.

5. Measure the quilt through the center from top to bottom and from side to side. Cut two striped strips to each measurement.

6. Sew the longer strips to the sides of the quilt. Press the seams toward the strips.

7. Sew a 6¼" red print #1 square to both ends of each shorter strip. Press the seams toward the strips. Sew strips to the top and bottom edges of the quilt; press.

FINISHING

Refer to pages 90–95 of "Basic Quiltmaking Techniques" as needed.

1. Mark the quilt top with a quilting design of your choice.

2. Cut the backing fabric crosswise into two equal lengths, remove the selvages, and sew the pieces together to make a backing with a vertical seam. Trim the backing so that it is approximately 6" larger than the quilt top.

3. Layer the quilt top with the batting and backing; baste.

4. Hand or machine quilt as desired.

5. Trim the excess batting and backing even with the edges of the quilt top and attach a hanging sleeve, if desired. Join the red print #2 binding strips with diagonal seams; bind the edges of the quilt.

6. Label your quilt.

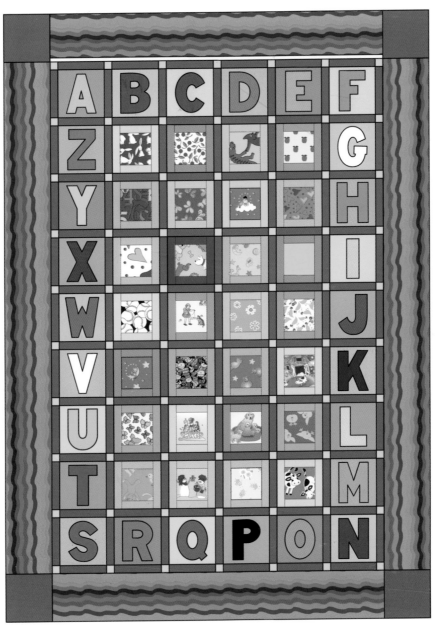

Quilt Layout

Appliqué Patterns

Patterns are reversed for fusible appliqué; no seam allowances are included.

Enlarge patterns 267%.
Cut 1 of each letter.

Appliqué Patterns

Patterns are reversed for fusible appliqué;
no seam allowances are included.

Enlarge patterns 267%.
Cut 1 of each letter.

BED BUGS

By Mimi Dietrich, Baltimore, Maryland, 2003.
Machine quilted by Laurie Gregg, Ellicott City, Maryland.

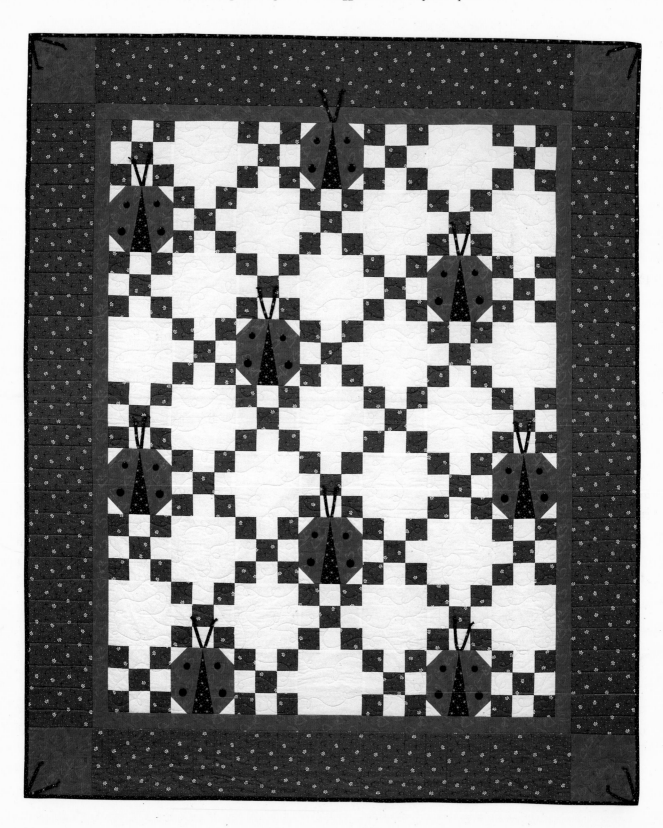

When Mimi's dad tucked the children in at night, he would always say "Good night! Sleep tight! Don't let the bed bugs bite!" The bugs won't bite if they are these fun ladybugs with three-dimensional antennae. Many little children fall asleep hugging a quilt and twirling the edges between their fingers, so Mimi thought it would be fun to include the "twirlers" in the quilt. Make this quilt as a special comfort to your toddler.

Finished quilt size: 57½" x 69½"
Finished block size: 6"

MATERIALS

Yardages are based on 42"-wide fabric.

2½ yards of green ladybug print for Nine Patch blocks and outer border

1¾ yards of white-on-white print for Nine Patch blocks and setting squares

1¼ yards of bright red print for Ladybug blocks and inner border

1 yard of black print for Ladybug blocks, antennae, and binding

3⅝ yards of fabric for backing

64" x 76" piece of batting

54 black buttons

Note: If you embellish your quilt with buttons, use it as a wall hanging rather than on the crib or toddler's bed. For a bed quilt, use an alternative such as fabric paint or markers.

CUTTING

All measurements include ¼"-wide seam allowances.

From the white-on-white print, cut: ✓

- 8 strips, 2½" x 42"
- 4 strips, 6½" x 40"; crosscut into 22 squares, 6½" x 6½"
- 3 strips, 3" x 40"; crosscut into 36 squares, 3" x 3"

From the *lengthwise* grain of the green ladybug print, cut:

- 2 border strips, 6½" x 57½"
- 2 border strips, 6½" x 45½"

From the remaining green ladybug print, cut: ✓

- 10 strips, 2½" x 40"

5 from each green

From the black print, cut: ✓

- 2 strips, 3" x 40"; crosscut into 9 rectangles, 3" x 6½"
- 7 binding strips, 2" x 40"
- 13 strips, 1" x 10"

From the bright red print, cut: ✓

- 8 border strips, 2" x 40"
- 1 strip, 6½" x 40"; crosscut into 4 squares, 6½" x 6½"
- 4 strips, 4" x 40"; crosscut into 18 rectangles, 4" x 8"

MAKING NINE PATCH BLOCKS

You need 32 Nine Patch blocks. Refer to "Making Strip Sets" on page 85 as needed.

1. Sew a 2½"-wide white-on-white strip between two 2½"-wide green strips; press. Make four strip sets. Crosscut into 64 segments, each 2½" wide.

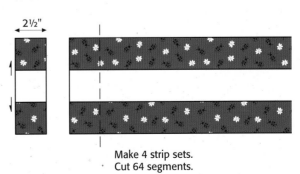

Make 4 strip sets.
Cut 64 segments.

39

2. Sew a 2½"-wide green strip between two 2½"-wide white-on-white strips; press. Make two strip sets. Crosscut into 32 segments, each 2½" wide.

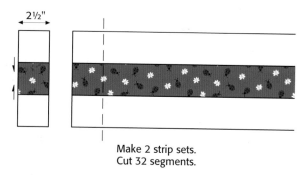

Make 2 strip sets.
Cut 32 segments.

3. Sew a segment from step 2 between two segments from step 1; press. Make 32.

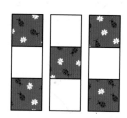
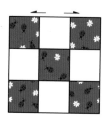

Make 32.

PAPER PIECING
LADYBUG BLOCKS

You need nine Ladybug blocks. For more detailed information on paper piecing, see Carol Doak's *Easy Machine Paper Piecing* (That Patchwork Place, 1994).

1. Trace the pattern on page 42 onto lightweight paper. Make nine tracings. Cut out each pattern on the dashed line. (We don't recommend photocopying, as this may distort the pattern. If you *must* photocopy, check that the copied design measures exactly 6½" square.)

2. Hold a paper pattern wrong (unmarked) side up to a light source. Position a 3" x 6½" black rectangle right side up over the center (piece 1). Pin in place.

3. Place a 4" x 8" red rectangle (piece 2) right sides together with the black rectangle as shown. Make sure the fabrics extend ¼" past the line between pieces 1 and 2; pin.

4. Turn the pattern marked side up, and sew on the line between pieces 1 and 2. Use a very small stitch (20 stitches per inch) and a large needle (size 90). Trim the seam allowance to ¼".

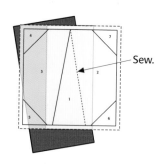

Sew.

5. Fold piece 2 open and press flat.

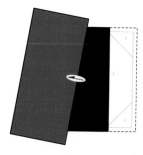

6. Add pieces 3–7 in order in the same fashion to complete the block. Use a 4" x 8" red rectangle for piece 3, and use 3" white-on-white squares for pieces 4–7. Make nine.

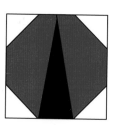

Make 9.

7. Use a ruler and rotary cutter to trim each block even with the outside edge of the paper pattern. Remove the paper foundations.

8. Fold the long edges of each 1"-wide black strip right sides together and sew a ¼" seam. Use a loop turner to turn the strips right side out. If you prefer, fold both edges to the center and topstitch.

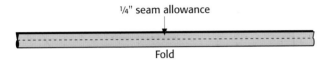

¼" seam allowance

Fold

Granny's Goodies

A loop turner is a great tool for turning strips. Look for it in the notions aisle of any sewing store.

9. Tie two knots 6" apart in each strip as shown. Trim the ends of the strip up to the knots. Make 13. Set four aside for the quilt corners.

6"

Make 13.

10. Fold the knotted strips in half and sew them to the top of each Ladybug block as shown.

ASSEMBLING THE QUILT

1. Arrange the Nine Patch, Ladybug, and 6½" white-on-white blocks in nine rows of seven blocks each as shown in the quilt layout at right.

2. Sew the blocks together in rows; press the seams toward the Nine Patch blocks.

3. Sew the rows together. Press the seams toward the bottom of the quilt so that the antennae fold away from the bugs.

4. Sew the red strips end to end with diagonal seams to make one continuous border strip. Measure the quilt through the center from top to bottom and cut two strips to that measurement. Sew the strips to the sides of the quilt. Press the seams toward the strips.

5. Measure the quilt through the center from side to side, including the strips you've just added. Cut two strips to that measurement and sew them to the top and bottom of the quilt; press.

6. Sew the 6½" x 57½" green strips to the sides of the quilt. Press the seams toward the green strips.

7. Sew a 6½" red square to both ends of each 6½" x 45½" green strip. Press the seams toward the strips. Sew to the top and bottom edges of the quilt; press.

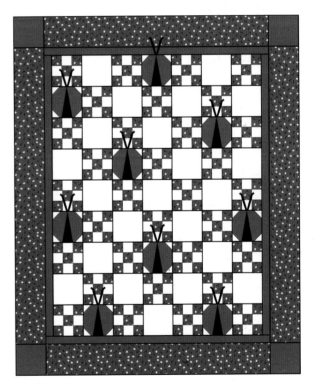

Quilt Layout

FINISHING

Refer to pages 90–95 of "Basic Quiltmaking Techniques" as needed.

1. Mark the quilt top with a quilting design of your choice.

2. Cut the backing fabric crosswise into two equal lengths, remove the selvages, and sew the pieces together to make a backing with a horizontal seam. Trim the backing so that it is approximately 6" larger than the quilt top.

3. Layer the quilt top with the batting and backing; baste.

4. Hand or machine quilt as desired.

5. Trim the excess batting and backing even with the edges of the quilt top and attach a hanging sleeve, if desired. Join the black binding strips with diagonal seams; bind the edges of the quilt.

6. Refer to the photo on page 38 and sew four black buttons to each Ladybug block. Make sure they are attached securely. Sew the four remaining black antennae to the corners of the quilt.

7. Label your quilt.

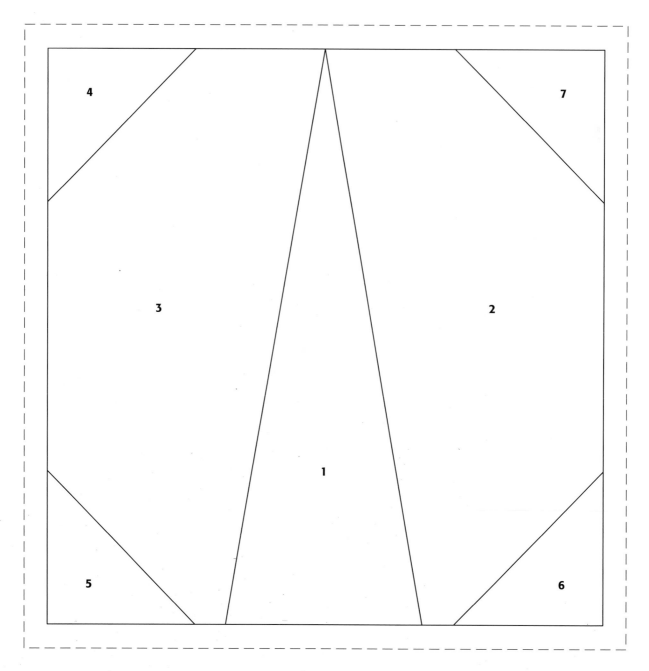

Foundation Pattern
Make 9.

TREASURE BASKETS

Designed by Mimi Dietrich, Baltimore, Maryland, 2003. Pieced by Norma Campbell, Arnold, Maryland, and machine quilted by Linda Newsom, Crofton, Maryland.

It's fun to have special places to keep your treasures. Each basket on this quilt has a pocket for notes, small stuffed animals, or the treasures that every child loves to collect. Use cheerful 1930s-style print fabrics to brighten up a little girl's room.

Finished quilt size: 64¼" x 89¾"

Finished block size: 9"

MATERIALS

Yardages are based on 42"-wide fabric.

6 yards of yellow print for Basket blocks, border blocks, and setting triangles

3 fat quarters *each* of assorted pink, green, violet, and blue 1930s-style prints for Basket blocks and border blocks

⅝ yard blue 1930s-style print for binding

5½ yards of fabric for backing

71" x 96" piece of batting

5" square of template plastic

48 pastel-colored buttons

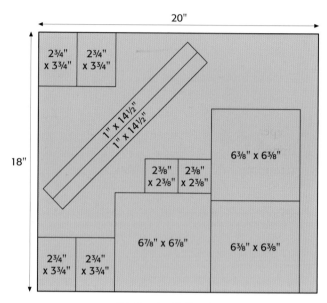

Fat-Quarter Cutting Layout

CUTTING

All measurements include ¼"-wide seam allowances.

Note: Each fat quarter makes two Basket blocks. Refer to the cutting layout above right.

From *each* fat quarter, cut:

- 2 bias strips, 1" x 14½" (24 total)
- 1 square, 6⅞" x 6⅞"; cut once diagonally to yield 2 half-square triangles (24 total)
- 2 squares, 6⅜" x 6⅜" (24 total)
- 2 squares, 2⅜" x 2⅜"; cut once diagonally to yield 4 half-square triangles (48 total)
- 4 rectangles, 2¾" x 3¾" (48 total; you will have 8 left over.)

From the yellow print, cut:

- 10 strips, 2" x 40"; crosscut into 48 rectangles, 2" x 6⅞"
- 2 strips, 3⅞" x 40"; crosscut into 12 squares, 3⅞" x 3⅞". Cut once diagonally to yield 24 half-square triangles.

- 3 strips, 9⅞" x 40"; crosscut into 12 squares, 9⅞" x 9⅞". Cut once diagonally to yield 24 half-square triangles.
- 3 strips, 2¾" x 40"; crosscut into 40 squares, 2¾" x 2¾"
- 8 strips, 5" x 40"; crosscut into 20 rectangles, 5" x 6"; 32 squares, 5" x 5"; and 4 rectangles, 5" x 9½"
- 4 strips, 9½" x 40"; crosscut into 15 squares, 9½" x 9½"
- 5 squares, 14" x 14"; cut twice diagonally to yield 20 quarter-square triangles
- 2 squares, 7¼" x 7¼"; cut once diagonally to yield 4 half-square triangles

From the ⅝ yard of blue 1930s-style print, cut:

- 9 binding strips, 2" x 40"

MAKING BASKET BLOCKS

You need 24 Basket blocks.

1. Sew a 2⅜" print triangle to a 2" x 6⅞" yellow rectangle as shown; press. Measure, mark, and carefully trim the opposite end of the rectangle at a 45° angle as shown. Make 24.

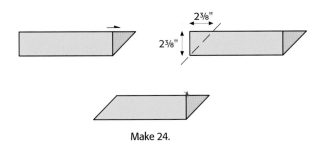

2⅜"
2⅜"
2⅜"

Make 24.

2. Repeat step 1, sewing a print triangle to the opposite end of a yellow print rectangle and trimming as shown; press. Make 24.

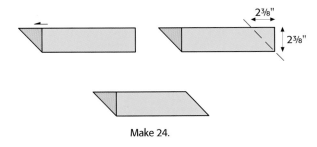

2⅜"
2⅜"

Make 24.

3. Fold a 6⅜" print square in half diagonally, right sides out. Place the folded square on the right side of a matching 6⅞" triangle, aligning the raw edges as shown. Baste the raw edges with a scant ¼" seam to make a triangle pocket. Make 24.

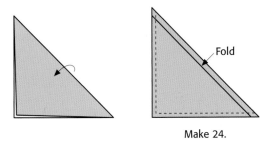

Fold

Make 24.

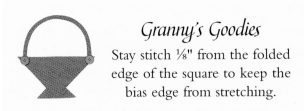

Granny's Goodies

Stay stitch ⅛" from the folded edge of the square to keep the bias edge from stretching.

4. Sew a unit from step 1 to the left edge of a matching unit from step 3 as shown; press. Sew a matching unit from step 2 to the right edge as shown; press. Make 24.

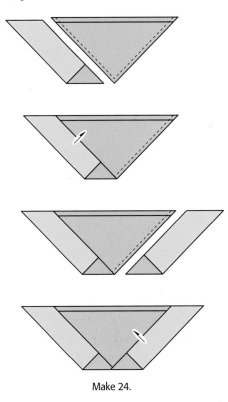

Make 24.

5. Sew a 3⅞" yellow triangle to each unit from step 4 as shown; press. Make 24.

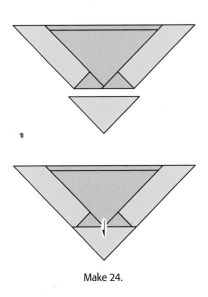

Make 24.

6. Use the placement guide on page 48 to trace the handle placement lines on each 9⅞" yellow triangle.

7. Fold the long edges of each 1"-wide bias strip to the center of the strip, wrong sides together, so that the raw edges meet. Baste along both folded edges with small stitches. Gently pull one of the threads to ease the strip into a curve.

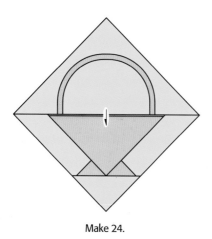

Pull thread to create curve.

8. Refer to the photo on page 43. Use a glue stick to position a handle on each marked 9⅞" triangle, curving the strip to fit. Appliqué the handle in place. Make 24.

9. Sew a unit from step 8 to a matching-colored unit from step 5 as shown; press. Take care that you do not sew the basket pocket closed in the seam. Make 24.

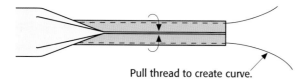

Make 24.

MAKING BORDER BLOCKS

You need 20 border blocks: 16 of block A and 4 of block B. These blocks use a quick-piecing technique Sally devised, called "Mary's Triangles," named for her friend Mary Kelleher.

1. Sew a 2¾" x 3¾" print rectangle to each 2¾" yellow square as shown; press. Make 40 total, 10 of each color.

Make 40 total
(10 of each color).

2. Arrange and sew a pink unit to each green unit from step 1 as shown. Repeat to sew violet units and blue units together in pairs as shown. Make 10 of each. Carefully clip the center seam in each unit; press as shown.

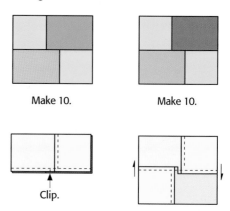

Make 10.   Make 10.

Clip.

3. Cut the 5" square of template plastic once diagonally. Align a triangle template with the corner of each unit from step 2 and trace the diagonal line as shown. Repeat on the opposite corner as shown. Mark all units.

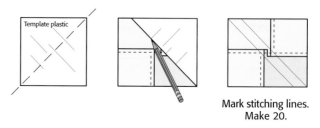

Mark stitching lines.
Make 20.

4. Place each unit from step 3 right sides together with a 5" x 6" yellow rectangle. Sew on the marked lines and cut between them as shown; press. Make 40.

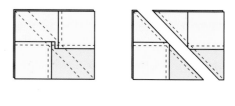

Make 40 total.

5. Arrange and sew one unit of each color from step 4 and two 5" yellow squares as shown; press. Make 16 and label them block A.

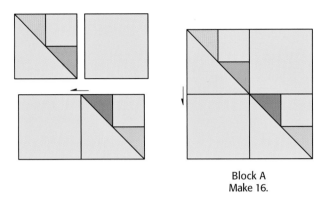

Block A
Make 16.

6. Arrange and sew one unit of each color from step 4 and one 5" x 9½" yellow rectangle as shown; press. Make four and label them block B.

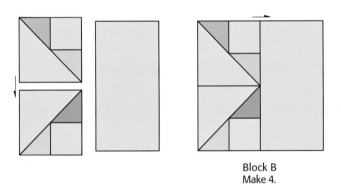

Block B
Make 4.

ASSEMBLING THE QUILT

1. Arrange the Basket blocks, 9½" yellow squares, A and B border blocks, yellow quarter-square side setting triangles, and yellow half-square corner setting triangles as shown in the quilt layout above right.
2. Sew the blocks and setting triangles together in diagonal rows. Press the seams in opposite directions from row to row.
3. Sew the rows together; press.

FINISHING

Refer to pages 90–95 of "Basic Quiltmaking Techniques" as needed.

1. Mark the quilt top with a quilting design of your choice.

Quilt Layout

2. Cut the backing fabric crosswise into two equal lengths, remove the selvages, and sew the pieces together to make a backing with a vertical seam. Trim the backing so that it is approximately 6" larger than the quilt top.
3. Layer the quilt top with the batting and backing; baste.
4. Hand or machine quilt as desired.
5. Trim the excess batting and backing even with the edges of the quilt top and attach a hanging sleeve, if desired. Join the blue print binding strips with diagonal seams; bind the edges of the quilt.
6. Sew buttons at the end of each basket handle.
7. Label your quilt.

Granny's Goodies
Hide special notes or treasures in the baskets for your child when you give the quilt away.

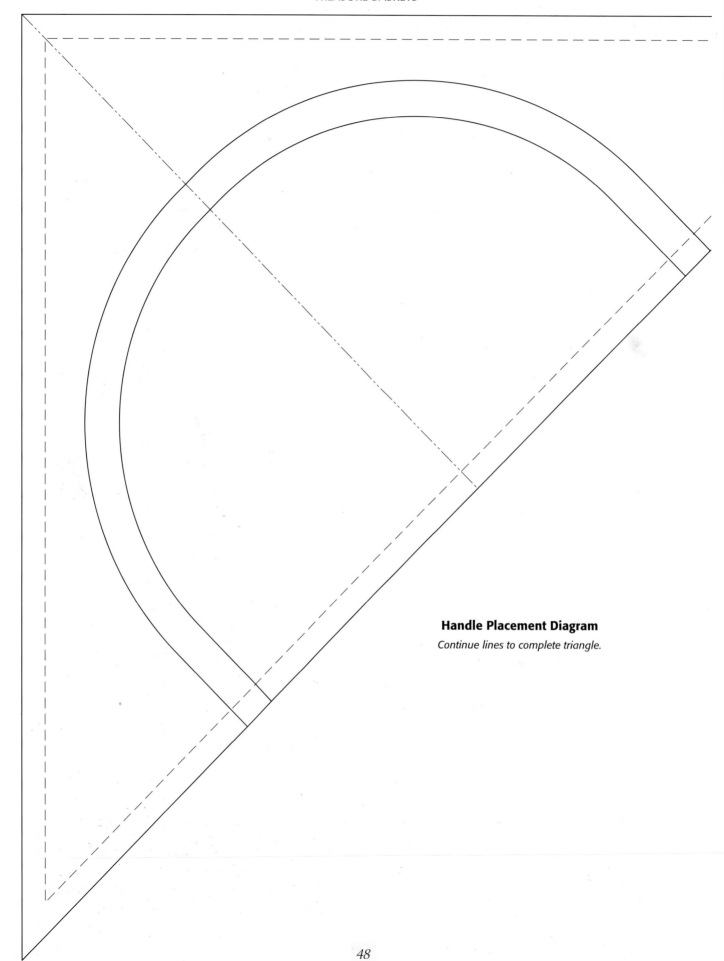

Handle Placement Diagram
Continue lines to complete triangle.

FANTASY FISHES

By Mimi Dietrich, Baltimore, Maryland, 2003.
Machine quilted by Laurie Gregg, Ellicott City, Maryland.

When Mimi's son Ryan was about 10 years old, he spent the summer digging a hole for a goldfish pond. It became a "Tom Sawyer" experience when his friends wandered by and stayed to dig. To commemorate the event, Mimi made Ryan a fish quilt. The original quilt was made with some of the first hand-dyed fabrics she purchased; this one is made with batiks to give the illusion of water and sunlight.

Finished quilt size: 65½" x 78¼"
Finished block size: 9"

MATERIALS

Yardages are based on 42"-wide fabric.

3¼ yards of light blue batik for blocks, setting triangles, and binding

2⅝ yards of dark blue batik for blocks and outer border

¾ yard of bright orange batik for blocks and inner border

¾ yard of medium orange batik for blocks

½ yard of gold batik for blocks

4¾ yards of fabric for backing

72" x 85" piece of batting

3½" square of template plastic

12 dark blue buttons (¾") for large fish eyes

20 dark blue buttons (⅜") for small fish eyes

CUTTING

All measurements include ¼"-wide seam allowances.

From the bright orange batik, cut:
- 8 border strips, 1½" x 40"
- 1 strip, 2⅜" x 40"; crosscut into 10 squares, 2⅜" x 2⅜"
- 2 strips, 3⅞" x 40"; crosscut into 18 squares, 3⅞" x 3⅞"

From the *lengthwise* grain of the dark blue batik, cut:
- 2 border strips, 6½" x 66¼"
- 2 border strips, 6½" x 65½"

From the remaining dark blue batik, cut:
- 10 strips, 2" x 40". Set 8 strips aside. From 2 strips, cut 20 rectangles, 2" x 3".
- 1 strip, 2⅜" x 40"; crosscut into 10 squares, 2⅜" x 2⅜"

From the medium orange batik, cut:
- 2 strips, 3½" x 40"; crosscut into 10 rectangles, 3½" x 4½"
- 2 strips, 3⅞" x 40"; crosscut into 18 squares, 3⅞" x 3⅞"
- 2 strips, 3½" x 40"; crosscut into 12 squares, 3½" x 3½"

From the light blue batik, cut:
- 4 strips, 3½" x 40". Set 2 strips aside. From 2 strips, cut 40 rectangles, 2" x 3½".
- 4 strips, 6½" x 40". Set 2 strips aside. From 2 strips, cut 40 rectangles, 2" x 6½".
- 3 strips, 3⅞" x 40"; crosscut into 30 squares, 3⅞" x 3⅞"
- 4 squares, 14" x 14"; cut twice diagonally to yield 16 quarter-square triangles
- 2 squares, 7¼" x 7¼"; cut once diagonally to yield 4 half-square triangles
- 8 binding strips, 2" x 40"

From the gold batik, cut:
- 3 strips, 3⅞" x 40"; crosscut into 30 squares, 3⅞" x 3⅞"

MAKING FISH CHAIN BLOCKS

You need 20 Fish Chain blocks. These blocks use a quick-piecing technique Sally devised, called "Mary's Triangles," named for her friend Mary Kelleher.

1. Draw a diagonal line on the wrong side of each 2⅜" bright orange square. Place each marked square right sides together with a 2⅜" dark blue square. Make 10. Stitch ¼" on each side of the line. Cut on the drawn line; press. Make 20.

Mark.   Stitch.   Cut.   Press.
         Make 10.   Trim corners.
                            Make 20.

2. Sew each unit from step 1 to a dark blue rectangle as shown; press. Make 20.

Make 20.

3. Sew two units from step 2 together as shown. Clip the center seam; press as shown. Make 10.

Clip.

Make 10.

4. Cut the 3½" square of template plastic once diagonally. Align a triangle template with the corner of each unit from step 3 and trace the diagonal line as shown. Repeat on the opposite corner. Mark all units.

 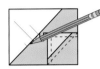

Mark stitching lines.

5. Place each unit from step 4 right sides together with a medium orange rectangle. Make 10. Sew on the marked lines and cut between them as shown; press. Make 20.

Make 10.   Make 20.

6. Sew a unit from step 5 between two 2" x 3½" light blue rectangles as shown; press. Make 20.

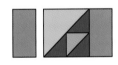 

Make 20.

7. Sew a 3½"-wide light blue strip between two 2"-wide dark blue strips; press. Make two strip sets. Crosscut the strip sets into 40 segments, each 2" wide.

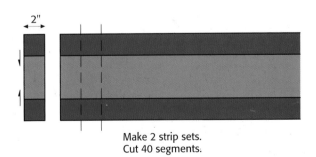

Make 2 strip sets.
Cut 40 segments.

8. Sew each unit from step 6 between two segments from step 7; press. Make 20.

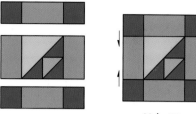

Make 20.

9. Sew each unit from step 8 between two 2" x 6½" light blue rectangles as shown; press. Make 20.

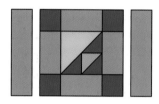
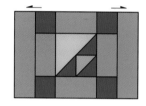

Make 20.

10. Sew a 6½"-wide light blue strip between two 2"-wide dark blue strips; press. Make two strip sets. Crosscut the strip sets into 40 segments, each 2" wide.

2"

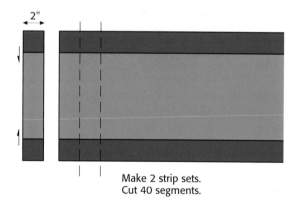

Make 2 strip sets.
Cut 40 segments.

11. Sew a unit from step 9 between two segments from step 10; press. Make 20.

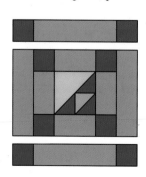
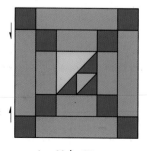

Make 20.

MAKING LARGE FISH BLOCKS

You need 12 large Fish blocks.

1. Draw a diagonal line on the wrong side of each 3⅞" medium orange square. Place each marked square right sides together with a 3⅞" bright orange square. Make 18. Stitch ¼" on each side of the line. Cut on the drawn line; press. Make 36.

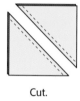

Stitch.
Make 18.
Cut.
Press.
Trim corners.
Make 36.

2. Repeat step 1 with the 3⅞" gold squares and 3⅞" light blue squares. Make 60.

Stitch.
Make 30.
Cut.
Press.
Trim corners.
Make 60.

3. Arrange a 3½" medium orange square, three units from step 1, and five units from step 2 as shown. Sew the units and squares into rows; press. Sew the rows together; press. Make 12.

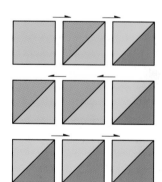
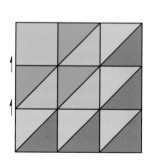

Make 12.

ASSEMBLING THE QUILT

1. Arrange the Fish Chain blocks, large Fish blocks, quarter-square side setting triangles, and half-square corner setting triangles as shown in the quilt layout below. Rotate the Fish Chain block in the lower-right corner so that the fish is swimming in the opposite direction.

2. Sew the blocks and setting triangles together in diagonal rows. Press the seams in opposite directions from row to row.

3. Sew the rows together; press.

4. Sew the bright orange strips together in pairs with diagonal seams to make four border strips. Measure the quilt through the center from top to bottom, and cut two strips to that measurement. Sew the strips to the sides of the quilt. Press the seams toward the strips.

5. Measure the quilt through the center from side to side, including the strips you've just added. Cut two strips to that measurement and sew them to the top and bottom of the quilt; press.

6. Sew the 6½" x 66¼" dark blue strips to the sides of the quilt, and the 6½" x 65½" dark blue strips to the top and bottom. Press the seams toward the dark blue strips.

FINISHING

Refer to pages 90–95 of "Basic Quiltmaking Techniques" as needed.

1. Mark the quilt top with a quilting design of your choice.

2. Cut the backing fabric crosswise into two equal lengths, remove the selvages, and sew the pieces together to make a backing with a vertical seam. Trim the backing so that it is approximately 6" larger than the quilt top.

3. Layer the quilt top with the batting and backing; baste.

4. Hand or machine quilt as desired.

5. Trim the excess batting and backing even with the edges of the quilt top and attach a hanging sleeve, if desired. Join the light blue binding strips with diagonal seams; bind the edges of the quilt.

6. Refer to the photo on page 49 and sew a button eye on each fish.

7. Label your quilt.

Quilt Layout

SUMMER CAMP

By Sally Schneider, Albuquerque, New Mexico, 2003.
Machine quilted by Kate Sullivan, Puyallup, Washington.

This quilt—reminiscent of carefree summers spent hiking, swimming, fishing, or just having fun outdoors—will please any young person in your family. Choose five blue-to-purple prints, ranging from dark to light, for the sky and water. Add six assorted green prints for the trees, and four prints each for the fish and flying geese. Try flannel fabrics to make a quilt that is warm and cozy all year-round.

Finished quilt size: 67½" x 82½"

Finished block size: 10"

Granny's Goodies

Flannel fabrics can shrink more than other fabrics, so they often measure less than 40" wide when washed. They also are thicker and require wider binding strips. The materials list and cutting directions take this into account.

MATERIALS

Note: This quilt uses four blue prints, ranging from dark (#1) to light (#4). See "Granny's Goodies" above regarding fabric widths.

1⅞ yards of light background print for Tree blocks

1¾ yards of dark blue-green print for outer border and binding

1¼ yards *total* of assorted green prints for Tree blocks

1¼ yards of blue print #2 (dark medium) for Mountain blocks, Fish blocks, Fish triangles, and corner setting triangles

1¼ yards of blue print #3 (light medium) for Mountain blocks, Flying Geese blocks, and side setting triangles

⅔ yard of brown print for Tree blocks and inner border

⅔ yard of blue print #1 (dark) for Mountain blocks and side setting triangles

½ yard of outdoor print for Tree blocks and side setting triangles

⅜ yard *total* of assorted dark prints for Flying Geese blocks

⅜ yard *total* of assorted gold prints for Fish blocks

⅜ yard of blue print #4 (light) for Mountain blocks

¼ yard of purple print for Mountain blocks

5 yards of fabric for backing

74" x 89" piece of batting

CUTTING

Note: You will cut the larger pieces (e.g., setting triangles, borders) first. Use the remaining fabric to cut pieces for blocks. Cutting for each block is listed separately. Some fabrics are used more than once.

SETTING TRIANGLES

From blue print #1, cut:
- 1 square, 16" x 16"; cut twice diagonally to yield 4 quarter-square triangles. (You will have 2 extra triangles.)

From blue print #3, cut:
- 1 square, 16" x 16"; cut twice diagonally to yield 4 quarter-square triangles. (You will have 1 extra triangle.)

From the outdoor print, cut:
- 1 square, 16" x 16"; cut twice diagonally to yield 4 quarter-square triangles

From blue print #2, cut:
- 1 square, 8½" x 8½"; cut once diagonally to yield 2 half-square triangles

BORDERS AND BINDING

From the brown print, cut:
- 8 border strips, 2" x 38"

From the dark blue-green print, cut:
- 8 border strips, 4¼" x 38"
- 9 binding strips, 2½" x 38"

MOUNTAIN BLOCKS

From *each* of blue prints #1–#4, cut:
- 4 strips, 1¾" x 22" (16 total)

From the purple print, cut:
- 1 strip, 5½" x 38"; crosscut into 4 squares, 5½" x 5½"

TREE BLOCKS

From the brown print, cut:
- 3 strips, 1" x 38"

From the light background print, cut:
- 3 strips, 4⅝" x 38"; crosscut into 18 squares, 4⅝" x 4⅝"
- 28 strips, 1¾" x 38". Crosscut into the following pieces (cut the larger pieces first; then cut the smaller pieces from the leftover strips):
    - 42 rectangles, 1¾" x 10½"
    - 42 rectangles, 1¾" x 8"
    - 42 rectangles, 1¾" x 2½"
    - 42 squares, 1¾" x 1¾"

From the outdoor print, cut:
- 4 squares, 4⅝" x 4⅝"

From the assorted green prints, cut a *total* of:
- 21 strips, 1¾" x 38"

FISH BLOCKS

From the assorted gold prints, cut a *total* of:
- 1 strip, 3⅜" x 38"; crosscut into 8 squares, 3⅜" x 3⅜"
- 2 strips, 3" x 38"; crosscut into 15 squares, 3" x 3"

From blue print #2, cut:
- 3 strips, 3" x 38"; crosscut into 30 squares, 3" x 3"
- 1 strip, 3⅜" x 38"; crosscut into 8 squares, 3⅜" x 3⅜"
- 1 square, 8½" x 8½"; cut once diagonally to yield 2 half-square triangles
- 2 squares, 8⅜" x 8⅜"; cut twice diagonally to yield 8 quarter-square triangles
- 3 squares, 5½" x 5½"

FLYING GEESE BLOCKS

From blue print #3, cut:
- 4 strips, 4½" x 38"; crosscut into 28 squares, 4½" x 4½"

From the assorted dark prints, cut a *total* of:
- 14 rectangles, 4½" x 8½"

MAKING MOUNTAIN BLOCKS

You need four Mountain blocks.

1. Sew a 1¾"-wide blue print #1 strip to a 5½" purple square as shown. Trim the strip even with the edges of the square; press. Sew the trimmed strip to the adjacent side of the unit; trim and press. Make four.

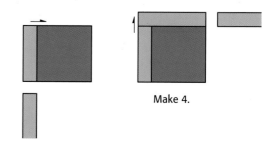

Make 4.

2. Repeat step 1 with 1¾"-wide strips of blue print #2, #3, and #4 as shown. Make four.

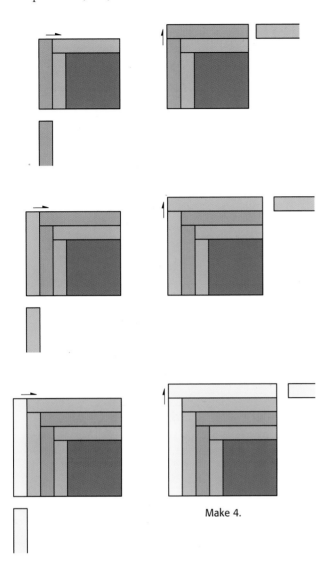

Make 4.

MAKING TREE BLOCKS

You need 21 Tree blocks: 14 of Tree block A and 7 of Tree block B.

1. Turn both long edges of each 1"-wide brown strip under ¼" and press. Use matching-colored thread to topstitch the strips over 11 of the 4⅝" light background squares as shown. Cut the squares apart.

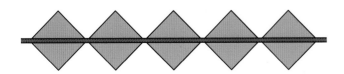

2. Draw a diagonal line on the wrong side of each square from step 1, intersecting the "trunk." Place each marked square right sides together with a remaining light background square and stitch ¼" on each side of the line. Cut on the drawn line; press. Make 14.

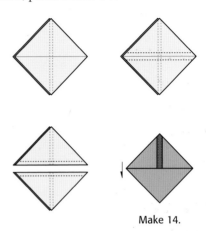

Make 14.

3. Repeat step 2 with the 4⅝" outdoor print squares. Make seven. (You will have one extra unit.)

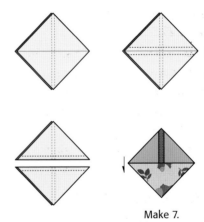

Make 7.

4. Identify the sides of the squares from step 2 and step 3 as shown. Stitch a 1¾"-wide green strip to side 1 of each square. Trim the strip even with the edges of the square; press. Sew the trimmed strip to side 2 of the unit; trim and press. Repeat with all the squares from steps 2 and 3.

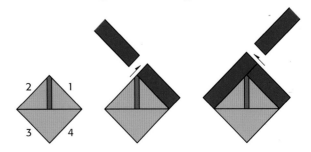

5. Sew the leftover green strips (from step 4) between two 1¾" light background squares as shown; press.

6. Repeat step 4 to stitch a matching green strip from step 5 to each square as shown; press.

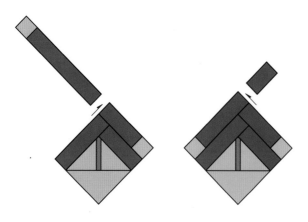

7. Sew the leftover green strips (from step 6) between two 1¾" x 2½" light background rectangles as shown; press.

8. Repeat step 4 to stitch a matching green strip from step 7 to each square as shown; press.

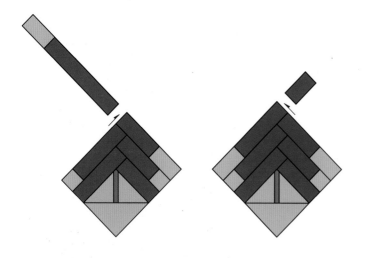

9. Referring to step 4 on page 57 as needed, sew a 1¾" x 8" light background rectangle to side 2 and side 4 of each square as shown; press. Sew a 1¾" x 10½" light background rectangle to side 1 and side 3; press. Label the 14 blocks with the background-base Tree block A, and the seven blocks with the outdoor-print-base Tree block B.

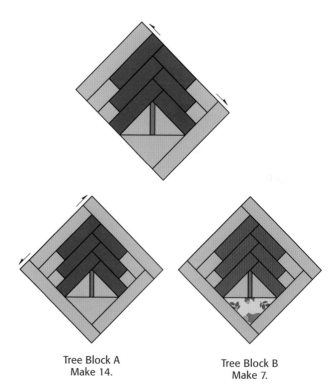

Tree Block A
Make 14.

Tree Block B
Make 7.

MAKING FISH UNITS, BLOCKS, AND SETTING TRIANGLES

You need 15 fish units. They will be used to make three Fish blocks, two Fish side setting triangles (C), and two Fish corner setting triangles (D).

1. Draw a diagonal line on the wrong side of each 3⅜" gold square. Place each marked square right sides together with a 3⅜" blue print #2 square. Make eight. Stitch ¼" on each side of the line. Cut on the drawn line; press. Make 16.

Make 16.

2. Arrange a unit from step 1, two 3" blue print #2 squares, and a 3" matching gold print square as shown. Sew the unit and squares into rows; press. Sew the rows together; press. Make 15 fish units. (You will have one extra unit from step 1.)

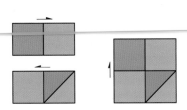

Make 15.

3. Arrange three units from step 2 and one 5½" blue print #2 square as shown. Sew the units and squares into rows; press. Sew the rows together; press. Make three Fish blocks.

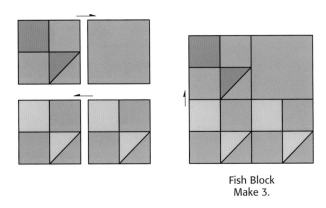

Fish Block
Make 3.

4. Arrange a unit from step 2 with two blue print #2 quarter-square triangles as shown. Sew the unit and triangles together; press. Make two and label them C.

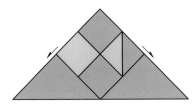

Fish Side Setting Triangle C
Make 2.

5. Arrange two units from step 2 with two blue print #2 quarter-square triangles and one blue print #2 half-square triangle as shown. Make one of each arrangement. Sew the units and triangles together; press. Label them D.

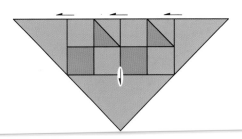

Fish Corner Setting Triangle D
Make 1.

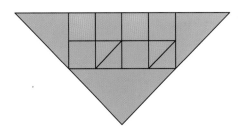

Fish Corner Setting Triangle D
Make 1.

MAKING FLYING GEESE BLOCKS

You need 14 Flying Geese blocks.

1. Refer to "Sewing Folded Corners" on page 85. Sew a 4½" blue print #3 square to each end of a 4½" x 8½" print rectangle as shown; trim and press. Make 14.

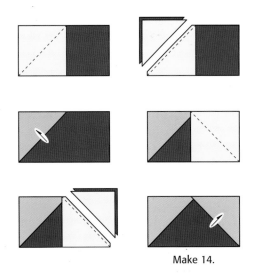

Make 14.

2. Arrange the blocks in a horizontal row as shown. Sew the blocks together; press.

59

ASSEMBLING THE QUILT

1. Arrange the Mountain, Tree, and Fish blocks; the blue print #1, blue print #3, and outdoor print quarter-square side setting triangles; and the Fish side setting triangles (C) in diagonal rows as shown.

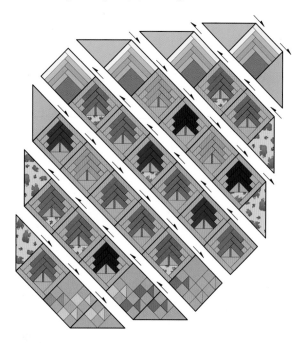

2. Sew the blocks and setting triangles together in diagonal rows; press. (Note that the triangles are oversized so the center design appears to "float.")

3. Sew the rows together; press.

4. Refer to the photo on page 54 and the quilt layout at right. Sew the Fish corner setting triangles (D) and the blue print #2 half-square corner setting triangles to the quilt. Press the seams toward the corner setting triangles.

5. Use a rotary cutter and ruler to carefully trim the edges of the quilt, making sure to allow for the ¼" seam allowance.

6. Refer to the photo and layout. Sew the Flying Geese row to the top edge of the quilt, easing as necessary. Press the seams away from the Flying Geese row.

ADDING BORDERS

1. Sew the brown border strips together end to end with diagonal seams to make one continuous border strip. Measure the quilt through the center from top to bottom and cut two strips to that measurement. Sew the strips to the sides of the quilt. Press the seams toward the strips.

2. Measure the quilt from side to side, including the strips you've just added. Cut two strips to that measurement and sew them to the top and bottom of the quilt; press.

3. Repeat steps 1 and 2 to piece, measure, cut, and sew the 4¼"-wide blue-green strips to the sides, top, and bottom of the quilt. Press the seams toward the blue-green strips.

Quilt Layout

FINISHING

Refer to pages 90–95 of "Basic Quiltmaking Techniques" as needed.

1. Mark the quilt top with a quilting design of your choice.

2. Cut the backing fabric crosswise into two equal lengths, remove the selvages, and sew the pieces together to make a backing with a vertical seam. Trim the backing so that it is approximately 6" larger than the quilt top.

3. Layer the quilt top with backing and batting; baste.

4. Hand or machine quilt as desired.

5. Trim the excess batting and backing even with the edges of the quilt top and attach a hanging sleeve, if desired. Join the blue-green binding strips with diagonal seams; bind the edges of the quilt.

6. Label your quilt.

Butterfly Kisses

By Mimi Dietrich, Baltimore, Maryland, 2003.
Machine quilted by Linda Newsom, Crofton, Maryland.

How delightful it is to watch butterflies flutter around the flowers in a colorful garden!
These bright butterflies will bring a garden of sweet dreams to any young girl who
shares a butterfly kiss with Mom and Dad—or Grandma!—at bedtime each night.

Finished quilt size: 63½" x 81½"
Finished block size: 9"

Granny's Goodies

Teach your child the secret of a butterfly kiss: flutter your eyelashes against her cheek so she can feel the soft kiss of a butterfly.

MATERIALS

Yardages are based on 42"-wide fabric.

3¾ yards of sky-blue print for Butterfly blocks, setting squares, and border blocks

1½ yards of multicolored butterfly print for border blocks

¾ yard of bright blue print for butterfly appliqués, flower appliqués, and binding

½ yard of bright green print for butterfly and leaf appliqués

⅜ yard *each* of bright value prints in pink, purple, yellow, and orange for butterfly and flower appliqués

¼ yard *each* of light value prints in pink, purple, and blue for butterfly and flower appliqués

¼ yard of light green print for butterfly appliqués

5 yards of fabric for backing

70" x 88" piece of batting

2 skeins of light brown embroidery floss

CUTTING

All measurements include ¼"-wide seam allowances. See below and pages 63 and 64 for appliqué cutting instructions.

From the sky-blue print, cut:

- 9 strips, 9½" x 40"; crosscut into 35 squares, 9½" x 9½"
- 7 strips, 6" x 40"; crosscut into 24 rectangles, 6" x 9½", and 4 squares, 6" x 6"

From the multicolored butterfly print, cut:

- 1 strip, 9½" x 40"; crosscut into 4 squares, 9½" x 9½"
- 6 strips, 6½" x 40"; crosscut into 24 rectangles, 6½" x 9½"

From the bright blue print, cut:

- 8 binding strips, 2" x 40"

APPLIQUÉING THE BUTTERFLY BLOCKS

Mimi fused the appliqués to the background and finished the edges with the buttonhole stitch on her sewing machine. You can use your favorite technique. Refer to "Appliqué" on pages 86–88 as needed and adapt the patterns as necessary.

1. Use the patterns on page 65 to make templates for the butterfly appliqués (A–E). Cut four A and four B *each* from the bright pink, blue, and orange prints; three A and three B *each* from the bright purple and green prints; four C, eight D, and eight E *each* from the light pink, light blue, and bright yellow prints; and three C, six D, and six E *each* from the light purple and green prints.

2. Use the butterfly pattern to center and trace the butterfly onto a 9½" sky-blue square. Note that the butterfly is placed diagonally on the block. Make 18.

3. Refer to the photo on page 61 and the quilt layout on page 64. Appliqué pieces A–E (in alphabetical order) to the blocks.

4. Refer to the pattern on page 65. Use two strands of light brown embroidery floss and a chain stitch to embroider the antennae.

Chain Stitch

APPLIQUÉING THE SCALLOPED-BORDER BLOCKS

The scalloped border is made from individual blocks. You need 28 blocks total: 24 of block A and 4 of block B.

1. Make a template for the block A scallop by tracing the pattern on page 66. As with the rest of the appliqués in this quilt, the scallop is fused in place, so the template will be the required size. You do not need to add seam allowances. Place the template on each 6½" x 9½" butterfly print rectangle as shown, trace the template, and cut the scallop. Make 24.

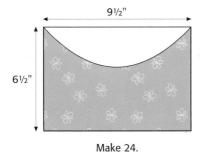

9½"

6½"

Make 24.

2. Place a scallop from step 1 over each 6" x 9½" sky-blue rectangle to make a 9½" square. Appliqué the scallop. Make 24 and label them block A.

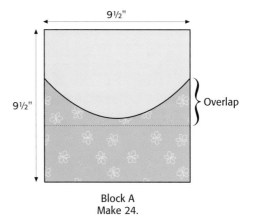

9½"

9½"

Overlap

Block A
Make 24.

3. Trim the sky-blue fabric ½" below the scalloped stitching to reduce bulk.

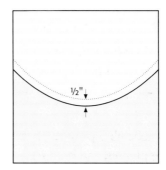

½"

4. Make a template for the block B scallop by tracing the pattern on page 66. The scallop is fused in place, so the template will be the required size. You do not need to add seam allowances. Place the template on each 9½" butterfly print square as shown, trace the template, and cut the scallop.

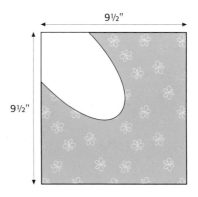

9½"

9½"

5. Place a scallop from step 4 over each 6" sky-blue square as shown. Appliqué the scallop. If desired, trim the excess sky-blue fabric. Make four and label them block B.

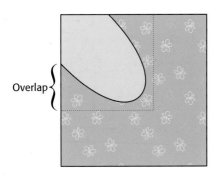

Overlap {

Block B
Make 4.

ASSEMBLING THE QUILT

1. Arrange the Butterfly blocks, 9½" sky-blue squares, and A and B border blocks in nine rows of seven blocks each as shown in the quilt layout below.

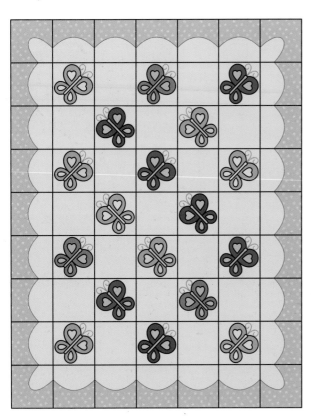

Quilt Layout

2. Sew the blocks together in rows. Press the seams away from the Butterfly blocks.

3. Sew the rows together; press.

APPLIQUÉING THE FLOWERS AND LEAVES

1. Use the patterns on page 66 to make templates for the flower, flower center, and leaf appliqués (F–H). Cut eight F *each* from the bright pink, purple, orange, and blue prints; eight G *each* from the light pink, light purple, light blue, and bright yellow prints; and 48 H from the bright green prints.

2. Refer to the photo on page 61. Appliqué the leaves (H) and then the flowers (F) and flower centers (G) on the borders where the scallops meet as shown.

FINISHING

Refer to pages 90–95 of "Basic Quiltmaking Techniques" as needed.

1. Mark the quilt top with a quilting design of your choice.

2. Cut the backing fabric crosswise into two equal lengths, remove the selvages, and sew the pieces together to make a backing with a vertical seam. Trim the backing so that it is approximately 6" larger than the quilt top.

3. Layer the quilt top with backing and batting; baste.

4. Hand or machine quilt as desired.

5. Trim the excess batting and backing even with the edges of the quilt top and attach a hanging sleeve, if desired. Join the bright-blue-print binding strips with diagonal seams; bind the edges of the quilt.

6. Label your quilt.

Appliqué Patterns

*Patterns are for fusible appliqué;
no seam allowances are included.*

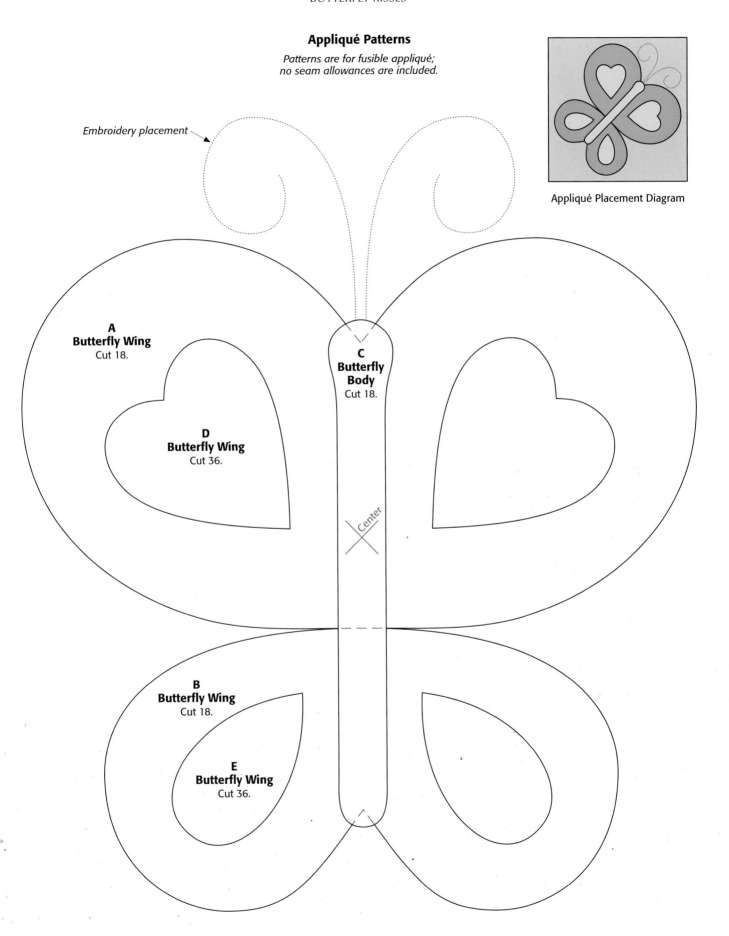

Appliqué Placement Diagram

Embroidery placement

**A
Butterfly Wing**
Cut 18.

**D
Butterfly Wing**
Cut 36.

**C
Butterfly
Body**
Cut 18.

Center

**B
Butterfly Wing**
Cut 18.

**E
Butterfly Wing**
Cut 36.

Appliqué and Scallop Patterns

No seam allowances are included.

H
Leaf
Cut 48.

G
Flower Center
Cut 32.

F
Flower
Cut 32.

Align with side of rectangle.

Block A Scallop
Cut 24.

Align with corner of square.

Block B Scallop
Cut 4.

HEARTS AND RIBBONS

By Sally Schneider, Albuquerque, New Mexico, 2003. Machine quilted by Kate Sullivan, Puyallup, Washington. Autographs collected by Lauren Daniel, Round Rock, Texas.

What teenage girl doesn't love hearts in all shapes, sizes, and forms, especially when combined with signature squares and stitched into an autograph quilt? These hearts are simple Four Patch blocks, and the twisted-ribbon border is constructed the "built-in" way—as blocks rather than as a separate border. When you sew the quilt top together, the border magically appears! Nothing could be more simple, or more sure to win a young lady's heart.

Finished Quilt Size: 63" x 84"

Finished Block Size: 5"

MATERIALS

Yardages are based on 42"-wide fabric.

4⅛ yards of cream print for Heart blocks, border blocks, and setting squares

1⅝ yards of dark teal print for border blocks and binding

¼ yard of light teal print for border blocks

¼ yard *each* of 9 assorted prints for Heart blocks

5 yards of fabric for backing

69" x 90" piece of batting

CUTTING

All measurements include ¼"-wide seam allowances.

From the cream print, cut:

- 12 strips, 3" x 40". Set 3 strips aside. From 6 strips, crosscut 18 strips, 3" x 13". From 3 strips, crosscut 34 squares, 3" x 3".
- 3 strips, 9" x 40"; crosscut into 10 squares, 9" x 9". Cut twice diagonally to yield 40 quarter-square triangles. (You will have 2 extra triangles.)
- 14 strips, 5½" x 40"; crosscut into 2 rectangles, 3" x 5½", and 90 squares, 5½" x 5½". Cut 2 squares once diagonally to yield 4 half-square triangles.

From *each* assorted print, cut:

- 2 strips, 3" x 40"; crosscut into 2 strips, 3" x 13" (18 total), and 8 rectangles, 3" x 5½" (72 total)

From the dark teal print, cut:

- 3 strips, 5½" x 40"; crosscut into 36 rectangles, 3" x 5½"
- 3 strips, 3" x 40"; crosscut into 38 squares, 3" x 3"
- 8 binding strips, 2¼" x 40"

From the light teal print, cut:

- 3 strips, 3" x 40"

MAKING HEART BLOCKS

You need 70 Heart blocks. This may sound like a lot, but they are so simple you can probably make them all in an afternoon. You've cut pieces to make 72 blocks; make them all and use the leftovers for the quilt label.

1. Sew a 3" x 13" cream strip to a 3" x 13" print strip as shown; press. Make 18 total, 2 of each print.

Make 18 total.

2. Crosscut each unit from step 1 into 4 segments, 3" wide. If you wish, layer several units, offsetting the top edges as shown, before cutting. Cut 72 segments total.

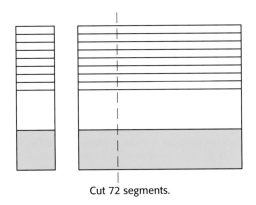

Cut 72 segments.

3. Sew a matching-colored 3" x 5½" print rectangle to each segment from step 2 as shown; press. Make 72.

Make 72.

MAKING BORDER BLOCKS

You will need a total of 76 border blocks in five variations: 2 each of block A and block B, 14 of block C, 20 of block D, and 38 of block E.

1. Sew a 3" x 40" cream strip to a 3" x 40" light teal strip; press. Make three strip sets. Crosscut them into two 5½"-wide segments and label them block A. Set the remaining strip sets aside for now.

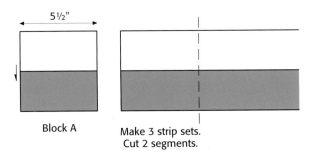

Block A

Make 3 strip sets.
Cut 2 segments.

2. Sew a 3" x 5½" dark teal rectangle to a 3" x 5½" cream rectangle; press. Make two and label them block B.

Block B
Make 2.

3. Crosscut the remaining strip sets from step 1 into 34 segments, 3" wide.

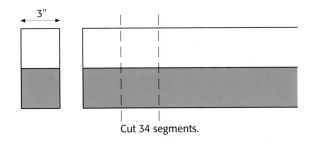

Cut 34 segments.

4. Refer to "Sewing Folded Corners" on page 85. Sew a 3" cream square to a 3" x 5½" dark teal rectangle as shown; trim and press. Make 14.

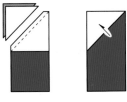

Make 14.

5. Sew a 3" cream square to a 3 " x 5½" dark teal rectangle, sewing the seam in the opposite direction as shown; trim and press. Make 20.

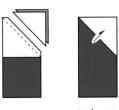

Make 20.

6. Sew a unit from step 4 to a segment from step 3 as shown; press. Make 14 and label them block C.

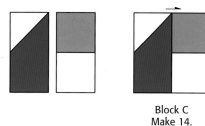

Block C
Make 14.

7. Sew a segment from step 3 to a unit from step 5 as shown; press. Make 20 and label them block D.

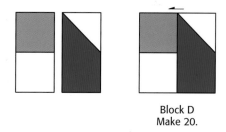

Block D
Make 20.

8. Sew a 3" dark teal square to a 9" cream quarter-square triangle as shown; trim and press. Make 38 and label them block E.

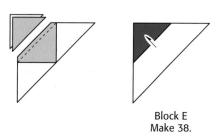

Block E
Make 38.

ASSEMBLING THE QUILT

1. Arrange the Heart blocks, 5½" cream squares, border blocks A–E, and four cream half-square corner triangles in diagonal rows as shown in the quilt layout above right.

2. Sew the blocks, squares, border blocks, and corner triangles together in diagonal rows. (Note that the triangles are oversized so the design appears to "float.") Press the seams toward the Heart blocks.

3. Sew the rows together; press.

4. Use a rotary cutter and ruler to carefully trim the edges of the quilt, making sure to allow for a ¼" seam allowance.

Quilt Layout

FINISHING

Refer to pages 90–95 of "Basic Quiltmaking Techniques" as needed.

1. Mark the quilt top with a quilting design of your choice.

2. Cut the backing fabric crosswise into two equal lengths, remove the selvages, and sew the pieces together to make a backing with a vertical seam. Trim the backing so that it is approximately 6" larger than the quilt top.

3. Layer the quilt top with the batting and backing; baste.

4. Hand or machine quilt as desired.

5. Trim the excess batting and backing even with the edges of the quilt top and attach a hanging sleeve, if desired. Join the dark teal binding strips with diagonal seams; bind the edges of the quilt.

6. Label your quilt.

PLAYING WITH PLAID

By Sally Schneider, Albuquerque, New Mexico, 2003.
Machine quilted by Linda Newsom, Crofton, Maryland.

Bright, cheery colors and cozy flannel fabrics make this quilt a cuddly keeper for any teenager, whether at home or off at college. Choose school colors, making sure to include both light and dark values, so that you can see the contrast. Simple strip piecing makes this quilt a quick and easy winner.

Finished quilt size: 68" x 90"

Finished block size: 10"

Granny's Goodies

Flannel fabrics can shrink more than other fabrics, so they often measure less than 40" wide when washed. They are also thicker and require wider binding strips. The materials list and cutting directions take this into account.

MATERIALS

See "Granny's Goodies" above regarding fabric widths.

3½ yards of blue print for blocks and border

2¼ yards of black print for blocks, sashing, and binding

1¾ yards of yellow print for blocks

1¼ yards of red print for blocks

1 yard of green print for blocks

¼ yard of black–and–white print for cornerstones

5¾ yards of fabric for backing

74" x 96" piece of batting

CUTTING

All measurements include ¼"-wide seam allowances.

From the yellow print, cut:
- 10 strips, 2½" x 38"
- 6 strips, 4½" x 38"

From the blue print, cut:
- 15 strips, 2½" x 38"

From the *lengthwise* grain of the blue print, cut:
- 4 border strips, 6¼" x 80"

From the red print, cut:
- 15 strips, 2½" x 38"

From the green print, cut:
- 10 strips, 2½" x 38"

From the black print, cut:
- 3 strips, 2½" x 38"
- 4 strips, 10½" x 38"; crosscut into 82 strips, 1½" x 10½"
- 9 binding strips, 2½" x 38"

From the black-and-white print, cut:
- 2 strips, 1½" x 38"; crosscut into 48 squares, 1½" x 1½"

MAKING PLAID BLOCKS

You need 35 Plaid blocks: 18 of block A and 17 of block B. Refer to "Making Strip Sets" on page 85 as needed.

1. Sew a 2½"-wide yellow strip between two 2½"-wide blue strips; press. Make five strip sets. Crosscut into 36 segments, each 4½" wide.

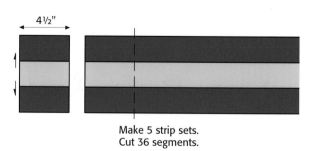

Make 5 strip sets.
Cut 36 segments.

72

2. Sew a 2½"-wide yellow strip between two 2½"-wide red strips; press. Make five strip sets. Crosscut into 34 segments, each 4½" wide.

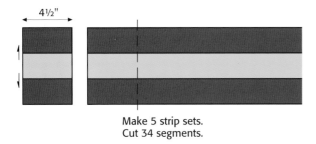

Make 5 strip sets.
Cut 34 segments.

3. Sew a 2½"-wide blue strip to a 2½"-wide green strip; press. Make five strip sets. Crosscut into 68 segments, each 2½" wide.

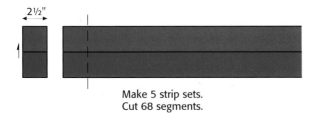

Make 5 strip sets.
Cut 68 segments.

4. Sew a 2½"-wide red strip to a 2½"-wide green strip; press. Make five strip sets. Crosscut into 72 segments, each 2½" wide.

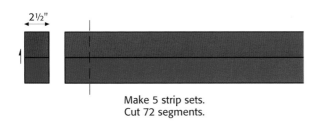

Make 5 strip sets.
Cut 72 segments.

5. Sew a 2½"-wide black strip between two 4½"-wide yellow strips; press. Make three strip sets. Crosscut into 35 segments, each 2½" wide.

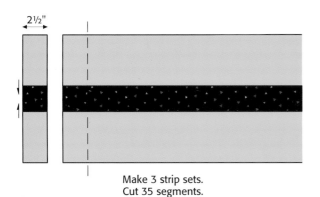

Make 3 strip sets.
Cut 35 segments.

6. Arrange two segments from step 1, four segments from step 4, and a segment from step 5 as shown. Sew the segments into rows; press. Sew the rows together; press. Make 18 and label them block A.

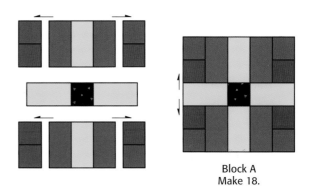

Block A
Make 18.

7. Arrange two segments from step 2, four segments from step 3, and a segment from step 5 as shown. Sew the segments into rows; press. Sew the rows together; press. Make 17 and label them block B.

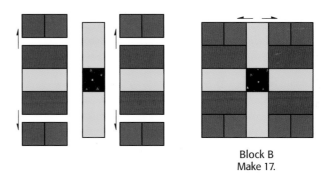

Block B
Make 17.

ASSEMBLING THE QUILT

1. Arrange three of block A, two of block B, and six 1½"-wide black strips to make a row. (Be sure the blocks are turned correctly.) Sew the blocks and strips into rows; press. Make four and label them row 1.

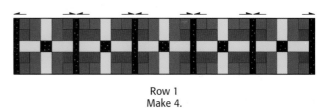

Row 1
Make 4.

2. Repeat step 1 with two of block A, three of block B, and six 1½"-wide black strips. Make three and label them row 2.

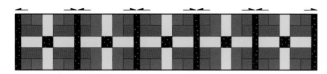

Row 2
Make 3.

3. Sew five 1½"-wide black strips and six black-and-white squares to make a row; press. Make eight and label them row 3.

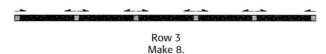

Row 3
Make 8.

4. Arrange the rows as shown in the quilt layout below. Sew the rows together; press.

5. Measure the quilt through the center from top to bottom and cut two 6¼"-wide blue strips to this measurement. Sew the strips to the sides of the quilt. Press the seams toward the strips.

6. Measure the quilt from side to side, including the strips you've just added. Cut two strips to that measurement and sew them to the top and bottom of the quilt; press.

FINISHING

Refer to pages 90–95 of "Basic Quiltmaking Techniques" as needed.

1. Mark the quilt top with a quilting design of your choice.

2. Cut the backing fabric crosswise into two equal lengths, remove the selvages, and sew the pieces together to make a backing with a vertical seam. Trim the backing so that it is approximately 6" larger than the quilt top.

3. Layer the quilt top with the batting and backing; baste.

4. Hand or machine quilt as desired.

5. Trim the excess batting and backing even with the edges of the quilt top and attach a hanging sleeve, if desired. Join the black binding strips with diagonal seams; bind the edges of the quilt.

6. Label your quilt.

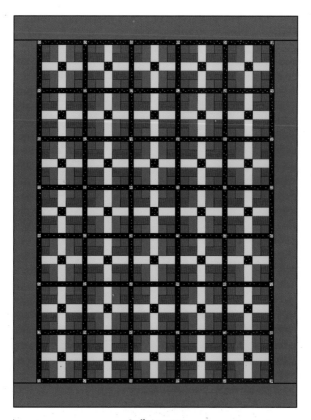

Quilt Layout

74

SCRAPBOOK MEMORIES

By Mimi Dietrich and Kaitlin Scott, Baltimore, Maryland, 2003.
Machine quilted by Laurie Gregg, Ellicott City, Maryland.

Photos hold such precious memories for all of us. As we look at them, we treasure special times and wonderful people. The beautiful papers we saw in our local scrapbooking store reminded both of us of quilt fabrics, inspiring this design. Why not gather favorite photos and make a scrapbook quilt for your student as he or she leaves home? With a quilt like this, you can wrap your student in memories.

Finished quilt size: 51½" x 64¼"

Finished block size: 9"

MATERIALS

Yardages are based on 42"-wide fabric.

2½ yards of pink floral print for Photo blocks, border blocks, and setting triangles

1¼ yards of blue print for Photo blocks and binding

1¼ yards of light pink print for Photo blocks and border blocks

¼ yard of black print for Photo blocks

3¼ yards of fabric for backing

58" x 71" piece of batting

18 photos, 4" x 6" (12 horizontally oriented and 6 vertically oriented)

9 commercial fabric sheets (see "Granny's Goodies" on page 77)

CUTTING

All measurements include ¼"-wide seam allowances.

From the black print, cut:

- 3 strips, 1¼" x 40"; crosscut into 72 squares, 1¼" x 1¼"

From the blue print, cut:

- 2 strips, 5⅝" x 40"; crosscut into 10 squares, 5⅝" x 5⅝". Cut once diagonally to yield 20 half-square triangles.
- 2 strips, 7⅛" x 40"; crosscut into 10 squares, 7⅛" x 7⅛". Cut once diagonally to yield 20 half-square triangles.
- 7 binding strips, 2" x 40"

From the light pink print, cut:

- 2 squares, 5⅝" x 5⅝"; cut once diagonally to yield 4 half-square triangles
- 2 squares, 7⅛" x 7⅛"; cut once diagonally to yield 4 half-square triangles
- 2 strips, 5" x 40"; crosscut into 14 squares, 5" x 5"
- 1 strip, 7¼" x 40"; crosscut into 10 rectangles, 2¾" x 7¼"
- 1 strip, 9½" x 40"; crosscut into 14 rectangles, 2¾" x 9½"

From the pink floral print, cut:

- 1 strip, 5⅝" x 40"; crosscut into 6 squares, 5⅝" x 5⅝". Cut once diagonally to yield 12 half-square triangles.
- 2 strips, 7⅛" x 40"; crosscut into 6 squares, 7⅛" x 7⅛". Cut once diagonally to yield 12 half-square triangles.
- 2 strips, 2¾" x 40"; crosscut into 18 squares, 2¾" x 2¾"
- 2 strips, 5" x 40"; crosscut into 18 rectangles, 2¾" x 5"
- 1 strip, 7¼" x 40"; crosscut into 10 rectangles, 2¾" x 7¼"
- 1 strip, 9½" x 40"; crosscut into 4 rectangles, 2¾" x 9½"
- 4 squares, 14" x 14"; cut twice diagonally to yield 16 quarter-square side setting triangles. (You will have 2 extra triangles.)
- 2 squares, 7¼" x 7¼"; cut once diagonally to yield 4 half-square corner setting triangles

MAKING THE PHOTO BLOCKS

You need 18 Photo blocks. Refer to "Granny's Goodies" below for tips on transferring photos to fabric.

Granny's Goodies

The modern granny can scan photos into her computer or use a digital camera. Print the photos on commercial fabric sheets prepared expressly for inkjet printers. We used a product called Printed Treasures, available from your local quilt shop or from Soft Fabric Photos (www.softfabricphotos.com, 303-716-9240).

When you transfer the photos, make sure to leave room to add ¼"-wide seam allowances around each image. The white edges become the seam allowances when you piece the blocks.

1. Refer to "Sewing Folded Corners" on page 85. Sew a 1¼" black square on each corner of each 4½" x 6½" photo transfer as shown; trim and press. Make 18.

2. Use the pattern on page 79 to make a template. Place the template on each blue, light pink, and pink floral 5⅝" triangle as shown. Mark and trim the triangles as shown. Cut 36 and label them piece A. Set the cutaway small triangles aside for another project.

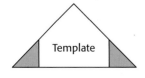

Cut 36.

3. Sew a matching piece A to the 4½" sides of each unit from step 1. Press the seams toward piece A. Make 18.

4. Sew each unit from step 3 between two matching 7⅛" triangles; press.

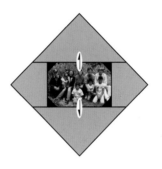

MAKING THE BORDER BLOCKS

You need a total of 14 border blocks: 10 of block A and 4 of block B.

1. Refer to "Sewing Folded Corners" on page 85. Sew a 2¾" pink floral square to the upper-left corner of each 5" light pink square as shown; trim and press. Make 10.

Make 10.

2. Sew a 2¾" x 5" pink floral rectangle to each unit from step 1 as shown; press. Make 10.

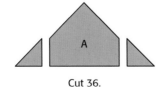
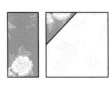
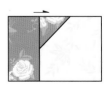

Make 10.

3. Sew a 2¾" x 7¼" pink floral rectangle to each unit from step 2 as shown; press. Make 10.

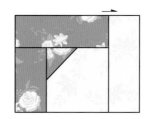

Make 10.

4. Sew a 2¾" x 7¼" light pink rectangle to each unit from step 3 as shown; press. Make 10.

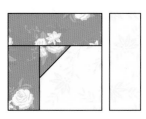

Make 10.

5. Sew a 2¾" x 9½" light pink rectangle to each unit from step 4 as shown; press. Make 10 and label them block A.

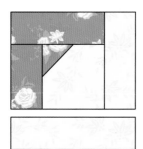

Block A
Make 10.

6. Refer to "Sewing Folded Corners" on page 85. Sew a 2¾" pink floral square to adjacent corners of a 5" light pink square as shown; trim and press. Make four.

Make 4.

7. Sew each unit from step 6 between two 2¾" x 5" pink floral rectangles as shown; press. Make four.

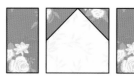

Make 4.

8. Sew each unit from step 7 between a 2¾" x 9½" pink floral rectangle and a 2¾" x 9½" light pink rectangle as shown; press. Make four and label them block B.

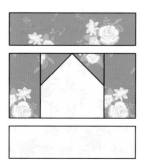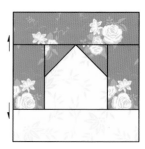

Block B
Make 4.

ASSEMBLING THE QUILT

1. Arrange the Photo blocks, A and B border blocks, quarter-square side setting triangles, and half-square corner setting triangles in diagonal rows as shown in the quilt layout on page 79. Make sure that all the photos are right side up!

2. Sew the blocks and setting triangles together in diagonal rows. Press the seams in opposite directions from row to row.

3. Sew the rows together; press.

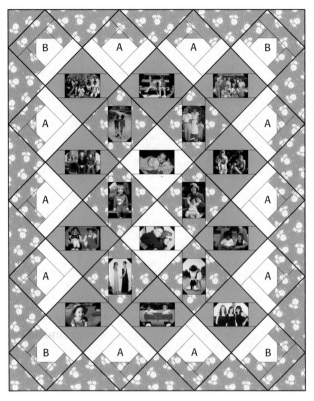

Quilt Layout

FINISHING

Refer to pages 90–95 of "Basic Quiltmaking Techniques" as needed.

1. Mark the quilt top with a quilting design of your choice.
2. Cut the backing fabric crosswise into two equal lengths, remove the selvages, and sew the pieces together to make a backing with a horizontal seam. Trim the backing so that it is approximately 6" larger than the quilt top.
3. Layer the quilt top with the batting and backing; baste.
4. Hand or machine quilt as desired.
5. Trim the excess batting and backing even with the edges of the quilt top and attach a hanging sleeve, if desired. Join the blue print binding strips with diagonal seams; bind the edges of the quilt.
6. Label your quilt.

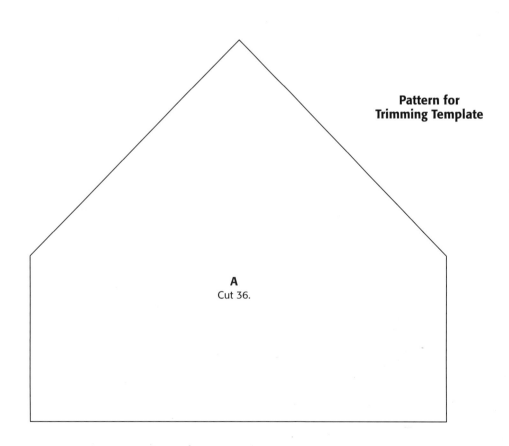

Pattern for Trimming Template

A
Cut 36.

DREAMWEAVER

By Sally Schneider, Albuquerque, New Mexico, 2003.
Machine quilted by Kate Sullivan, Puyallup, Washington.

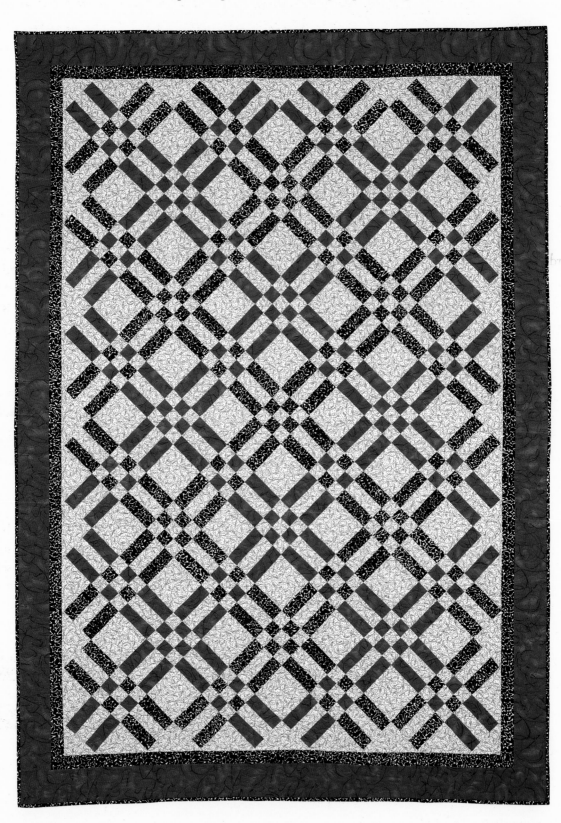

A simple combination of Rail Fence and Nine Patch blocks set on point produces this over-and-under, woven-look quilt. Make it in your child's school (or college) colors for a very special graduation gift that will help your student realize his or her dreams. Strong contrast between the background fabric and the two weaving colors brings the design to life.

Finished quilt size: 62" x 87½"

Finished block size: 4½"

MATERIALS

Yardages are based on 42"-wide fabric.

3 yards of black-and-white print for blocks, setting squares, and setting triangles

2⅛ yards of red print for blocks and outer border

2⅛ yards of black print for blocks, inner border, and binding

5¼ yards of fabric for backing

68" x 94" piece of batting

Granny's Goodies

Try a floral background for a more feminine quilt.

CUTTING

All measurements include ¼"-wide seam allowances.

From the black-and-white print, cut:

- 25 strips, 2" x 40"
- 5 strips, 5" x 40"; crosscut into 40 squares, 5" x 5". Cut 2 squares once diagonally to yield 4 half-square triangles.
- 3 strips, 8½" x 40"; crosscut into 9 squares, 8½" x 8½". Cut twice diagonally to yield 36 quarter-square triangles.

From the red print, cut:

- 17 strips, 2" x 40"
- 8 border strips, 4¼" x 40"

From the black print, cut:

- 26 strips, 2" x 40" (8 are for border)
- 8 binding strips, 2¼" x 40"

MAKING RAIL FENCE BLOCKS

You need 96 Rail Fence blocks: 48 *each* of Rail Fence A and Rail Fence B. Refer to "Making Strip Sets" on page 85 as needed.

1. Sew a 2"-wide black-and-white strip between two 2"-wide red strips; press. Make eight strip sets and label them strip set A. Set two strip sets aside. Crosscut the remaining six strip sets into 48 segments, 5" wide, and label them Rail Fence A.

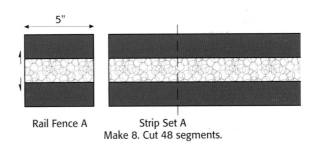

Rail Fence A

Strip Set A
Make 8. Cut 48 segments.

2. Sew a 2"-wide black-and-white strip between two 2"-wide black strips. Make seven strip sets and label them strip set B. Set one strip set aside. Crosscut the remaining six strip sets into 48 segments, 5" wide, and label them Rail Fence B.

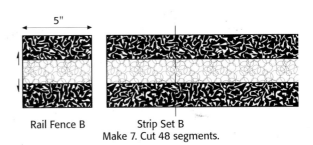

Rail Fence B

Strip Set B
Make 7. Cut 48 segments.

NINE PATCH BLOCKS

You need 39 Nine Patch blocks: 8 of Nine Patch A, 7 of Nine Patch B, and 24 of Nine Patch C.

1. Sew a 2"-wide red strip between two 2"-wide black-and-white strips to make a strip set; press. Crosscut into 16 segments, 2" wide.

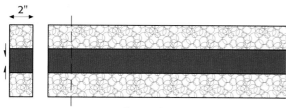

Make 1 strip set.
Cut 16 segments.

2. From the remaining two strip sets labeled A (see step 1 of "Making Rail Fence Blocks" on page 81), crosscut 32 segments, 2" wide.

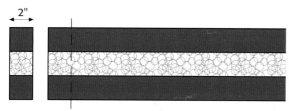

Cut 32 segments.

3. Sew a segment from step 2 between two segments from step 1; press. Make eight and label them Nine Patch A.

Nine Patch A
Make 8.

4. Sew a 2"-wide black strip between two 2"-wide black-and-white strips; press. Make four strip sets. Crosscut into 62 segments, 2" wide.

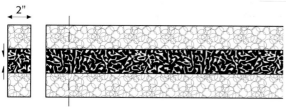

Make 4 strip sets.
Cut 62 segments.

5. Crosscut the remaining strip set labeled B (see step 2 of "Making Rail Fence Blocks" on page 81) into seven segments, 2" wide.

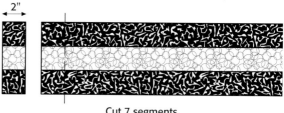

Cut 7 segments.

6. Sew a segment from step 5 between two segments from step 4; press. Make seven and label them Nine Patch B.

Nine Patch B
Make 7.

7. Sew a segment from step 2 between two segments from step 4; press. Make 24 and label them Nine Patch C.

Nine Patch C
Make 24.

ASSEMBLING THE QUILT

1. Arrange the Rail Fence and Nine Patch blocks, 5" black-and-white squares, quarter-square side setting triangles, and half-square corner setting triangles in diagonal rows as shown in the quilt layout on page 83. Be sure to turn the Nine Patch C blocks correctly to achieve the "woven" effect.

2. Sew the blocks, squares, and setting triangles together in diagonal rows. (Note that the triangles are oversized so the design appears to "float.") Press the seams in opposite directions from row to row.

3. Sew the rows together; press.

4. Use a rotary cutter and ruler to carefully trim the edges of the quilt, making sure to allow for a ¼" seam allowance.

5. Sew the eight remaining 2"-wide black strips end to end with diagonal seams to make one continuous border strip. Measure the quilt through the center from top to bottom and cut two strips to that measurement. Sew the strips to the sides of the quilt. Press the seams toward the strips.

6. Measure the quilt from side to side, including the strips you've just added. Cut two strips to that measurement and sew them to the top and bottom of the quilt; press.

7. Repeat steps 5 and 6 to piece, measure, fit, trim, and sew the red strips to the sides, top, and bottom of the quilt. Press the seams toward the red strips.

FINISHING

Refer to pages 90–95 of "Basic Quiltmaking Techniques" as needed.

1. Mark the quilt top with a quilting design of your choice.

2. Cut the backing fabric crosswise into two equal lengths, remove the selvages, and sew the pieces together to make a backing with a vertical seam. Trim the backing so that it is approximately 6" larger than the quilt top.

3. Layer the quilt top with the batting and backing; baste.

4. Hand or machine quilt as desired.

5. Trim the excess batting and backing even with the edges of the quilt top and attach a hanging sleeve, if desired. Join the black binding strips with diagonal seams; bind the edges of the quilt.

6. Label your quilt.

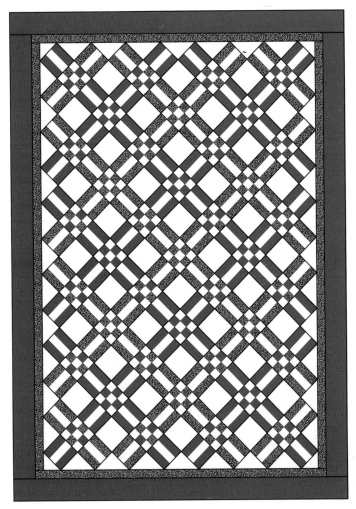

Quilt Layout

Basic Quiltmaking Techniques

The basic quiltmaking techniques in this section will help you complete any of the quilts in this book.

ROTARY CUTTING

The patchwork pieces for the quilts in this book are cut with a rotary cutter, cutting mat, and acrylic ruler.

To straighten the fabric for accurate cutting, fold your fabric in half lengthwise, with selvages parallel, on the cutting mat. Fold the fabric again, bringing the fold up to match the selvages.

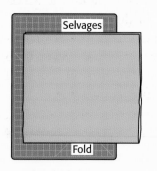

Fabric folded once

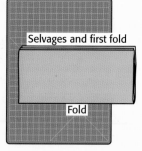

Fabric folded twice

Place a 6" square ruler on the fold nearest you, aligning it with the folded edge. Place a larger ruler (6" x 12" or 6" x 24") next to the square so that it covers the uneven edges of the fabric.

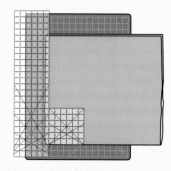

Align rulers.

Hold the long ruler, remove the 6" square, and make a clean cut along the ruler. Roll the rotary cutter away from you; use firm pressure.

Make a clean cut.

To cut strips, align the clean-cut edge of the fabric with the ruler marking for the desired strip width and cut a strip.

To cut squares or rectangles, cut a strip the desired measurement; then crosscut the strip into the desired shapes.

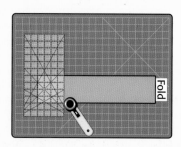

To cut two triangles from a square, cut a square the desired measurement. Place the ruler diagonally across the square and cut the square in half. The triangles have the straight of grain on the two short sides and the bias along the diagonal edge.

To cut four triangles from a square, cut a square the desired measurement. Cut the square twice diagonally. These triangles have the straight of grain along the long edge and bias edges on the two short sides.

CUTTING BIAS STRIPS

Cut bias strips by measuring an equal distance from a corner of your fabric. Place you ruler on these measurements and make a diagonal cut. Align your ruler with the desired strip width and cut strips.

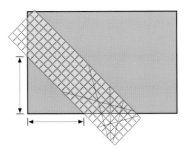

MACHINE PIECING

Many quilters use a sewing machine to sew patchwork, to piece together hand-appliquéd blocks, and to attach borders and binding.

SEWING ACCURATE SEAM ALLOWANCES

The most important skill for a quilter to master is making accurate ¼" seam allowances. You only have to be a little off to make a big difference in the way your pieces fit together. Test before you begin sewing. When you are sure that you are sewing a perfect ¼" seam, stick a piece of moleskin on your machine to use as a stitching guide.

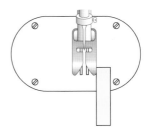

MAKING STRIP SETS

You can assemble many blocks or parts of blocks by cutting strips of fabric, sewing them together in a specific order to make a strip set, and then cutting the strip sets into segments.

1. Sew strips together in the order required for your design. Press the seams toward the darker fabric or as indicated in the quilt instructions. Use steam but press carefully to avoid stretching. Press from the right side first, and then from the wrong side to be sure that all the seam allowances face in the proper direction.

2. Carefully trim the uneven edge of the strip set, and then cut the required size and number of segments.

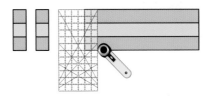

3. Join the segments to make the blocks or units required for your quilt.

SEWING FOLDED CORNERS

This method is great for adding a triangle to the corner of a square or rectangle. You work only with rectangles and squares. The measuring is simple, as is the sewing. You don't even need to draw a sewing line.

1. Place a piece of masking tape on your machine so that the right edge is in a straight line from the needle toward you. Extend the tape as far

forward as possible. Trim the tape away from the feed dogs.

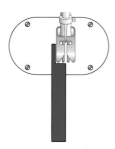

2. Place the small square on one corner of the large square or rectangle, right sides together and raw edges even. Begin sewing exactly in the corner of the top square. As you stitch, keep the opposite corner directly on the edge of the masking tape.

3. Trim the triangles ¼" from the seam; then press the triangle toward the corner.

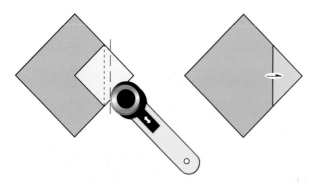

APPLIQUÉ

In an appliqué quilt, fabrics are applied on top of other fabrics instead of pieced together to make patchwork patterns. Curved designs can be accomplished easily with appliqué stitches.

BACKGROUND FABRIC

If the finished size of an appliqué block is 9" square, the background block needs to be cut 9½" square to allow for seams. Sometimes it is better to cut the square a bit larger at first, and then trim it to the correct size after the appliqué is complete. Appliqué background squares may be cut easily with a large square acrylic ruler and a rotary cutter.

In order to place the appliqué pieces on the background fabric accurately, mark the design on the background fabric.

Center the fabric right side up over the pattern. Trace the design carefully with a silver marking pencil. If your background fabric is too dark and you can't see the pattern clearly, you may need to trace it over a light box or a sunny window.

PREPARING APPLIQUÉS

Before sewing the appliqué fabrics to the background fabric, prepare the appliqués so that the seam allowances are turned under smoothly. Use freezer-paper templates to help you make perfectly shaped appliqués.

FREEZER-PAPER APPLIQUÉ

1. Place the freezer paper, coated side down, on your pattern, and trace the design with a sharp pencil. With repeated designs, such as flowers and leaves, make a plastic template to trace around. For one way designs, such as the angel on page 20, trace the pattern in reverse.

2. Cut out the freezer-paper shape on the pencil line. Do not add seam allowances.

3. Place the coated side of the freezer paper on the wrong side of the appliqué fabric. Iron the freezer paper to the fabric with a dry, hot iron.

Wrong side of fabric

Freezer paper

4. Cut out the appliqué shape, adding a ¼"-wide seam allowance around the outside of the freezer paper.

5. Baste the seam allowance over the freezer-paper edges. Clip any inside points, and fold outside points.

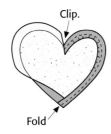

Clip.

Fold

6. Pin or baste the appliqué to the background fabric.

7. Stitch the appliqué to the background fabric with a traditional appliqué stitch (at right).

8. Once the shape is appliquéd, remove the basting stitches. Cut a small slit in the background fabric behind the appliqué and remove the freezer paper with tweezers.

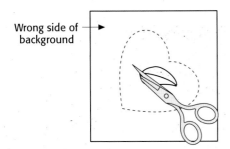

Wrong side of background

9. Press the appliqué from the wrong side to minimize flattening.

TRADITIONAL APPLIQUÉ STITCH

The traditional appliqué stitch is appropriate for sewing all areas of appliqué designs, including sharp points and curves.

Thread a needle with an 18"-long, single strand of thread; make a knot at one end. Slip your needle into the seam allowance from the wrong side of the appliqué piece, bringing it out along the fold line. This will hide the knot.

Stitch along the top edge of the appliqué. If you are right-handed, stitch from right to left. If you are left-handed, stitch from left to right.

Start the first stitch by moving your needle straight off the appliqué, inserting the needle into the background fabric.

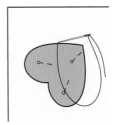

Let the needle travel under the background fabric parallel to the edge of the appliqué, bringing it up about ⅛" away from the last stitch along the pattern line. Pierce the edge of the appliqué piece, catching one or two threads of the folded edge.

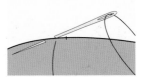

Move the needle straight off the appliqué into the background fabric. Let your needle travel under the background, bringing it up about ⅛" away from the last stitch, again catching the edge of the appliqué. Give the thread a slight tug and continue stitching. The stitching should be barely visible.

Try to keep the length of your stitches consistent as you stitch along the straight edges. Smaller stitches are sometimes necessary for curves and points.

FUSIBLE APPLIQUÉ

Combine fusible appliqué and machine stitches for a fast, easy, and durable way to make a child's appliqué quilt. Most of the projects in this book were made with this technique.

There are many different brands of fusible web on the market. Follow the manufacturer's directions carefully.

Fused shapes are cut the reverse of the design in the quilt. For instance, if a car faces left, it must be traced on the fusible web so that it faces right.

1. Trace the appliqué design on the paper backing of the fusible web.

2. Cut out the shape approximately ½" *outside* the pencil line.

3. On large shapes, also cut out the center of the design ¼" *inside* the pencil line. The appliqué will be fused along the edges and the center of the appliqué will remain soft.

4. Follow the manufacturer's directions to fuse the web to the wrong side of your fabric.

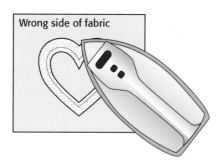
Wrong side of fabric

5. Cut out the appliqué piece on the pencil line.

6. Remove the paper backing, position the appliqué in place on the background fabric, and iron the appliqué in place.

7. Machine stitch around the outer edge of the appliqué with a satin stitch or buttonhole stitch.

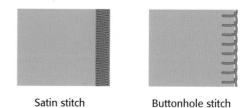

Satin stitch   Buttonhole stitch

QUILT-TOP ASSEMBLY

From setting blocks together to adding borders, you'll find details on assembling your quilt top here.

SQUARING UP BLOCKS

It may be necessary to "square up" your blocks before sewing them together to make the quilt top. Trim the edges with an acrylic ruler and a rotary cutter, leaving a ¼" seam allowance beyond any points or other important block details near the outside edges.

If you cut appliqué blocks larger than the size necessary, trim the blocks to size, including a ¼" seam allowance all around the outside.

STRAIGHT SETS

In straight sets, blocks are laid out in horizontal rows parallel to the edges of the quilt. There may be sashing strips between the blocks and corner squares where the sashing strips are joined. Lay the pieces out on a flat surface. Sew them together in rows;

then join the rows to complete the center of the quilt, pressing the seams as directed.

DIAGONALLY SET QUILTS

In diagonal sets, the blocks are laid out in diagonal rows and are at a 45° angle to the edges of the quilt. The spaces along the edge of a diagonally set quilt are filled with side setting and corner setting triangles. These triangles are cut so that the outside edge of the triangle is on the straight grain of the fabric to ensure that the edges won't stretch when you attach the border.

The directions for each quilt tell you how large to cut the triangles. In most cases, the triangles are intentionally cut larger than necessary and trimmed after the quilt top is completed. Place these side triangles in the spaces at the edge of your quilt; then piece them to the blocks as you sew the rows together. Follow the quilt plan for your particular quilt.

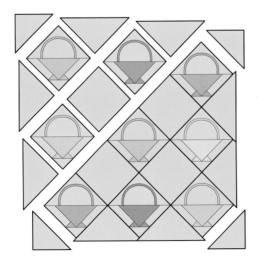

Granny's Goodies

Always sew with the triangles on the bottom to prevent stretching the bias edge.

Notice that the right-angle points of the triangles match the block edges, and the sharper points of the triangles extend beyond the edge of the block. Lay your ruler across the top of the block, keeping the edge of the ruler even with the raw edge of the block. Trim the triangles even with the raw edge.

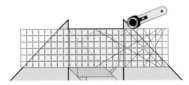

Once the quilt top is completed, square up the edges of the quilt, leaving a ¼"-wide seam allowance all around.

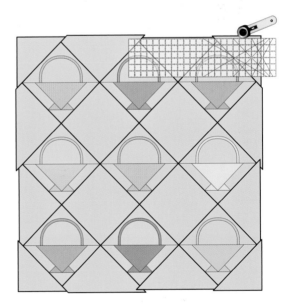

OVERLAPPED BORDERS

Borders add a finishing frame to your design. Cut your borders from the lengthwise grain of the fabric if possible. You can also cut them from the crosswise grain and piece the strips together with a diagonal seam (see page 93).

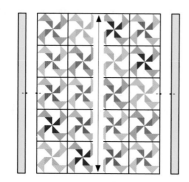

Overlapped Borders

The size of your finished quilt top can vary slightly from the stated size because of all the seams involved. For this reason, it's always a good idea to cut the borders to match your quilt. Measure the quilt through the center and cut the borders based on this measurement. Ease the edge of the quilt to fit the borders.

Measure center of quilt,
top to bottom.

Attach the long side borders first. Press the seams toward the border or toward the darker border when adding more than one border.

Next, stitch the top and bottom borders. Press the seam in the same direction as the first borders.

Measure center of quilt,
side to side, including borders.

MARKING THE QUILTING LINES

Quilting lines can follow the straight lines of patchwork in the quilt, outline the appliqué designs, or embellish spaces between the designs. It may not be necessary to mark the quilting designs if you are planning to quilt in the ditch (next to the seams) or if you are outlining patchwork pieces.

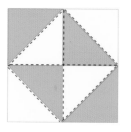

Quilting in the ditch

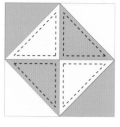

Outline quilting

For other types of quilting, however, you'll probably want to mark the quilting designs. Do this before basting the three layers together.

You can use a variety of tools to mark the quilting design onto the quilt top. Whichever tool you use for marking, test it on a sample of your fabric before using it on your quilt. Make sure you can see the lines, and make sure they can be removed.

To mark straight lines, use a yardstick or a long acrylic ruler. You can also use masking tape to mark straight lines. Simply quilt along the edges of the tape; then peel it off.

To mark more elaborate quilting designs, place the quilt top on top of the design and trace the design onto the fabric. Use a light box, or tape your work against a bright window if you have trouble seeing the design through the fabric. Another alternative is to use a precut plastic quilting stencil, readily available in quilt shops.

Machine quilters often use free-motion designs that do not need to be marked on the fabric.

BASTING

Before you begin to quilt, you must baste together the quilt top, batting, and backing. This secures the three layers for the quilting process.

1. Piece and press the quilt backing. Cut the backing at least 6" larger than the quilt top.
2. Place the backing on a smooth surface, right side down. Fasten the corners and sides of the fabric with masking tape.
3. Center and smooth the batting, and then the quilt top, on the backing. Pin the layers together in several places.
4. If you plan to hand quilt, use a long needle and light-colored basting thread. Start in the center and baste a large X in the center of the quilt; then baste parallel lines 4" to 6" apart to hold

the layers together. Finish by basting around the outside edges.

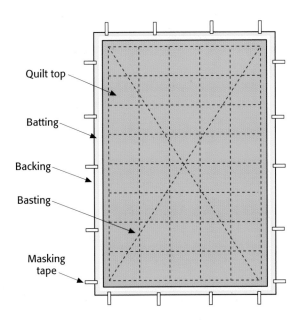

Quilt top
Batting
Backing
Basting
Masking tape

5. If you plan to machine quilt, use safety pins or a quilt-tacking tool to baste the layers together at 3" to 4" intervals.

QUILTING

After you complete your quilt top, the quilting stitches outline and define the pieces, create a design in the background, and add a wonderful texture to your quilt.

HAND QUILTING

Hand quilting stitches are short running stitches used to sew the front, batting, and backing of your quilt together.

Granny's Goodies

Hand quilt your heirloom quilts. Otherwise, for durability and washability, machine quilt.

1. Thread a Between quilting needle with an 18" length of hand-quilting thread and tie a single knot at the end of the thread. Insert the needle through the top layer of the quilt about ¾" from the point where you want to start stitching. Slide the needle through the batting and bring the needle out at the starting point.

2. Gently tug on the thread until the knot pops through the fabric and is buried in the batting. Take a backstitch and begin quilting, making a small running stitch that goes through all layers. Take two, three, or four stitches at a time, trying to keep them straight and even.

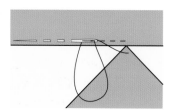

3. To end a line of quilting, make a single knot approximately ¼" from your quilt top. Take another backstitch into your quilt, tugging the knot into the batting layer and bringing the needle out ¾" away from your stitches. Clip the thread and let the end disappear into your quilt.

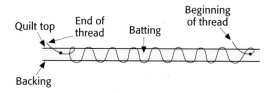

Quilt top
End of thread
Batting
Beginning of thread
Backing

MACHINE QUILTING

Quilts may be quilted quickly by machine. Adjust your stitch length so that it is a little longer than normal—approximately 10 stitches per inch. Test your machine by stitching on a sample to make sure that the thread tension is even on the top and bottom. Use a walking foot or even-feed foot on your machine to stitch straight lines, to outline borders, or to quilt in the ditch.

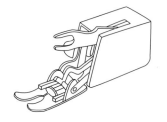 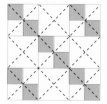

Walking or Even-Feed Foot

Free-motion quilting is used to fill in or embellish spaces between patchwork designs, to outline a motif in the fabric, or to stipple quilt. Use a darning foot and lower the feed dogs on your machine so that you can move the fabric freely. Practice on a sample before you actually sew on your quilt.

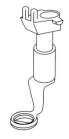 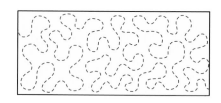

Darning Foot

HANGING SLEEVES

If you are planning to hang your quilts on a wall, sew a sleeve to the back before you apply the binding.

1. To make a 4"-wide sleeve, cut a strip of fabric 8½" wide and as long as the width of your quilt.

2. Turn under ¼" twice at each end of the strip and stitch a narrow hem.

8½"

3. Fold the sleeve lengthwise, wrong sides together, and pin the raw edges to the top of the quilt on the back side. Machine baste ⅛" from the top edge.

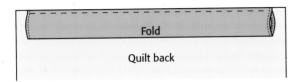

Fold

Quilt back

4. Sew the binding to the quilt; the raw edges of the sleeve will be covered when the binding is turned to the back of the quilt.

5. Pin the folded edge of the sleeve to the back of the quilt. Blindstitch the sleeve to the backing, being careful not to stitch through to the front of the quilt.

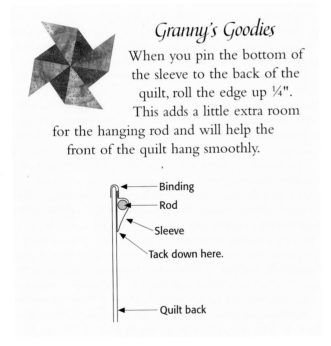

Granny's Goodies

When you pin the bottom of the sleeve to the back of the quilt, roll the edge up ¼". This adds a little extra room for the hanging rod and will help the front of the quilt hang smoothly.

Binding

Rod

Sleeve

Tack down here.

Quilt back

BINDING

Binding adds the finishing touch to your quilt. It is usually a good idea to use dark fabrics to frame your design, although if you want your binding to blend in, you can use the same fabric that you used for the outer border. Measure the distance around the quilt and add 10". Cut and sew enough strips of binding fabric to equal this measurement.

STRAIGHT-GRAIN BINDING

1. Cut strips across the width of fabric with a rotary cutter and an acrylic ruler.

Granny's Goodies

The dueling grannies! Mimi likes to cut 2"-wide strips for binding, while Sally prefers 2¼"-wide strips.

2. Sew the strips together with diagonal seams to create one long strip of binding. To make diagonal seams, cross two strip ends at right angles, right sides together. Lay these on a flat surface and imagine the strips as a large letter A. Draw a line across the crossed pieces to "cross the A," and then sew along the line. Your seam will be exact, and you can unfold a continuous strip.

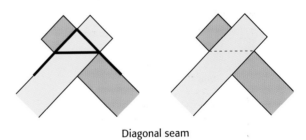

Diagonal seam

3. Trim the excess fabric, leaving a ¼"-wide seam allowance. Press the seam open to distribute the bulk.

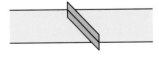

4. Fold the binding strip in half lengthwise, wrong sides together, and press with a hot steam iron.

APPLYING BINDING

1. Machine baste around the edge of the quilt to secure the three layers. Trim excess threads, batting, or backing even with the front of the quilt.

2. Starting 6" from a corner, align the raw edges of the binding with the raw edges of the quilt. Start sewing 4" from the end of the binding. Use a ¼" seam allowance.

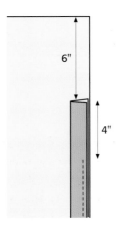

3. To miter the corner, stop stitching ¼" from the corner and backstitch.

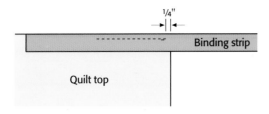

4. Fold the binding diagonally as shown so that it extends straight up from the second edge of the quilt.

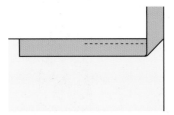

5. Fold the binding down, even with the second edge of the quilt. The fold should be even with the first edge. Resume sewing with a backstitch, ¼" from the fold. Repeat for the remaining corners. Stop stitching about 8" before the starting point.

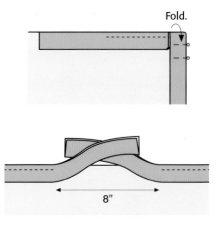

6. To connect the ends, fold the unstitched binding edges back on themselves so that they meet in the middle over the unsewn area of the quilt top. Press the fold.

7. Unfold both sides of the binding and with right sides together, match the centers of the pressed Xs. The right end should be on top of the left. Draw a diagonal line from the upper-left corner to the lower-right corner. Pin and stitch on the line.

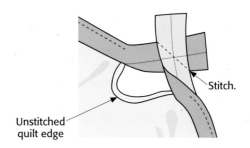

8. Trim the seam allowance to ¼" and press the seam open. Refold the binding, press the fold, and stitch the remainder of the binding.

9. Fold the binding over the edge of the quilt so that it covers the stitching on the back of the quilt. As you fold the corner, a folded miter will appear on the front.

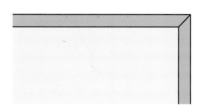

On the back, fold one side first, then the other, to create a miter on the back.

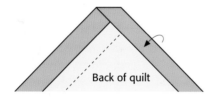

Back of quilt

10. Hand stitch the binding to the back of the quilt with the traditional appliqué stitch (see page 87). Hand stitch the diagonal fold.

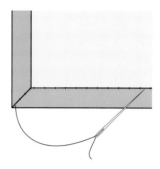

LABELS

You have made a very special quilt for a very special person. Make a label for the back of your quilt and sign your name and date. You will also want to include information about the quilt, such as a dedication or story about your quilt. We have included a label for you to trace.

Growing Up with Quilts

ABOUT THE AUTHORS

Mimi Dietrich started quilting almost 30 years ago when she made a baby quilt for her first son. While pregnant, she didn't know if she would have a boy or a girl, so she made a blue and yellow Sunbonnet Sue quilt and included Overall Bill—just in case! It was an appliquéd quilt, and Mimi has been appliquéing quilts ever since! She lives in Baltimore and loves the antique appliquéd quilts that were made in her hometown 150 years ago. Mimi has two sons, Jon and Ryan, and a daughter-in-law, Rachel, and looks forward to making "grand quilts" for her grandchildren. Mimi has written 10 books for Martingale & Company, including *Bed and Breakfast Quilts,* the best seller *Happy Endings,* and her personal favorite, *Baltimore Bouquets.*

Sally Schneider has been quilting since 1971, when she started making quilts for her children and for friends who were having babies. Since then she has made more than 300 quilts, mostly machine pieced, but she has two completely handmade quilts to her credit. She has lived all over the world, but she now calls Albuquerque, New Mexico, home. It's only a day's drive from her grandchildren in Austin, Texas!

Sally has three sons, David, Drew, and Ted; three daughters-in-law, Laura, Rashmi, and Carrie; and two grandsons, Zach and Alec—and she loves making quilts for them all. This is her sixth book for Martingale & Company; the others are on the subjects of scrap quilts and built-in, or "painless," borders. When she's not quilting, she enjoys landscape photography and singing in her church choir.